BIRMINGHAM CANALS

RAY SHILL

The History Press

First published 2013

The History Press
The Mill, Brimscombe Port
Stroud, Gloucestershire, GL5 2QG
www.thehistorypress.co.uk

British Library Cataloguing in Publication Data.
A catalogue record for this book is available from the British Library.

ISBN 978 0 7524 8856 1

Typesetting and origination by The History Press
Printed in Great Britain

Contents

Prologue to the Second Edition

The reprint was first suggested for 2011, but the final checks for *Silent Highways* and the subsequent promotion of that work, which deals with the construction of navigable waterways in the West and East Midlands, delayed the editing and updating of this second edition. The author has brought in new modern images, as well as additional archive images, to improve on the original text and update the work to include the changes of the last twelve years. Captions have been updated where necessary and historical data added through the result of new research. One image has required re-captioning as a result of correspondence and feedback following the publication of the first edition.

The sad loss of industrial heritage has continued, but in its place often sympathetic new development has enhanced the canal side and increased the popularity of the waterways as a boater's destination.

Acknowledgements

The original edition thanked various people and organisations for their help in providing information or images. While several contributors are now deceased, it remains important to recognise their contribution. Those acknowledged were as follows:

Aerofilms
Jeff Bennett, former boatman with Caggy Stevens
Birmingham Canal Navigations Society
Birmingham Public Libraries, Archives Department
Birmingham Public Libraries, Local Studies Department
Hugh Compton, Railway, Canal & Historical Society
Mike Constable
Steve Crook
George Dale
Alan Faulkner
Gloucester Waterways Museum
Roy Jamieson
Martin O'Keeffe
John Miller
National Waterways Museum, Ellesmere Port
Colin Scrivenor
Sandwell Public Libraries
John Whybrow
Worcester & Birmingham Canal Society

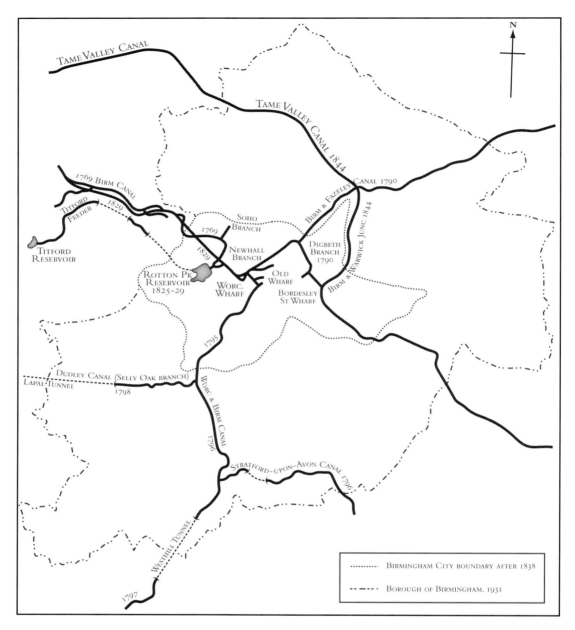

Canals of Birmingham. Birmingham grew from a small town to a great city within a period of 100 years. As Birmingham grew in size, more canals were encompassed within its boundaries.

Introduction

It is said that there are more miles of canals in Birmingham than in Venice. If all the canals within the City of Birmingham are taken into account, then this is probably a statement close to the truth. But if the old town of Birmingham is considered, the mileage is much less.

The canals contributed much to the growth of Birmingham through bringing coal and merchandise into the town. Birmingham was a small Warwickshire town which extended from Deritend, beside the River Rea, to the wild heath at Soho. From 1838 until 1931 Birmingham continued to grow in size, absorbing neighbouring communities. The greatest expansion happened in 1911 when Handsworth (Staffordshire), Aston Manor and Erdington (Warwickshire) and Kings Norton, Northfield and Yardley (Worcestershire) became part of the City of Birmingham.

Canal mileage from three counties was added to that which passed through the old town. Originally independent, canal companies were responsible for the construction and maintenance of these waterways. Today, the canal network is managed by the Canal & River Trust, whose local office at Ocker Hill serves Birmingham and the Black Country. Although part of one national network, each individual canal retains a separate identity. Birmingham is fortunate because most of the canals within its boundaries are still in water and regularly used.

It is the purpose of this book to look at all the canals within the city boundary and those in part of neighbouring Smethwick, which has several important canal features. Illustrations have been collected from a number of sources. Several have been published before, but it is the author's aim to show the diversity of the local canals and to compare the past with the present. There are ten separate waterways, which are listed under the company which constructed them, as follows:

Canal	Name of Canal Company
New Main Line	Birmingham Canal Navigations
Old Main Line	Birmingham Canal Navigations
Newhall Branch	Birmingham Canal Navigations
Birmingham & Fazeley	Birmingham Canal Navigations
Tame Valley	Birmingham Canal Navigations

Worcester & Birmingham	Worcester & Birmingham (Sharpness New Docks & Gloucester & Birmingham Navigation Co. from 1874)
Stratford upon Avon	Stratford upon Avon Canal Company (Oxford, Worcester & Wolverhampton Railway from 1856) (West Midland Railway from 1860) (Great Western Railway from 1863)
Dudley (No. 2)	Dudley Canal Company (Birmingham Canal Navigations from 1846)
Warwick & Birmingham	Warwick & Birmingham Canal Company (Grand Union Canal Company from 1929)
Birmingham & Warwick Junction	Birmingham & Warwick Junction Canal Company (Grand Union Canal Company from 1929)

A hundred years ago the Birmingham canal system was at its busiest, and even fifty years ago some wharves were kept busy with trade. There are several illustrations in this book which show this and the type of traffic then carried. During the 1930s there was even a mild resurgence in canal carrying when some new canal warehouses were constructed. The last fifty years, however, have seen a rapid decline in Midland canal carrying which has rendered most of the canal wharves and warehouses redundant.

There is now a rekindled interest in canals. People enjoy walking or boating along these waterways. But the canals of today are very different to those of the past. Gone are the muddy towpaths and the waterways crowded with working boats. Most of the factories and works that generated the canal trade have disappeared, and in their place are the waterside developments of the 1980s and 1990s which have completely transformed the Birmingham canal scene.

Many of the illustrations capture the old Birmingham canals of ninety or a hundred years ago when there was a busy trade on the canals. There are also those from the twilight years when canal carrying had all but ceased. Then there are the modern photographs which show the canal today, or ten years ago, sometimes picking out the surviving features from the old days. There is still a canal heritage, but every year another little bit is lost to the developers' whim.

The Birmingham Canal Navigations

The first canal to reach Birmingham was the Birmingham Canal Navigation (BCN), which linked the town of Birmingham with the Staffordshire & Worcestershire Canal at Aldersley Junction. The main reason for building this canal was to provide cheap coal for the workshops and factories of Birmingham. Wagonloads of coal collected from the existing coal mines around Bilston, Darlaston, West Bromwich and Wednesbury were brought along the turnpike road into Birmingham.

The turnpike trustees had the monopoly of the transport route and their rates reflected this. In January 1767 a group of prominent Birmingham citizens organised a public meeting at the White Swan in High Street, Birmingham. Their aim was to consider the possibility of forming a navigable canal to the local collieries. Those who attended set in motion a scheme to build the canal.

The proposal quickly developed from a simple canal from Birmingham to the collieries into a canal which joined other waterways then under construction. James Brindley was invited to survey a route from Birmingham to join another proposed canal, the Staffordshire & Worcestershire Canal, from Great Hayward to the River Severn. The first stretch of the Birmingham Canal was opened from Birmingham to collieries at Hill Top, West Bromwich, on 6 November 1769. It was then extended in stages until it reached Aldersley, on the Staffordshire & Worcestershire Canal, in 1772. When this canal was completed the BCN comprised the main line, 22⅝ miles long, which wound and turned through the Black Country. There was also a branch to the West Bromwich coal mines at Hill Top (the Wednesbury Canal). A flight of twenty, later twenty-one, locks brought the canal up from Aldersley to Wolverhampton, but then boatmen were subjected to another climb of three locks to the Smethwick Summit, with a further six down again to reach Birmingham. Water was in short supply and boats frequently grounded on some of the tight turns on the waterway.

The Birmingham Canal followed the contours of the land, although its course had been dictated by a number of factors. The route as originally surveyed by Brindley was some 6 miles shorter than that finally made. During the construction period there had been many occasions when the line of route had changed, often to favour certain mine owners. This in turn led to dissent and disagreement between the shareholders. Two groups had formed among their ranks, which held different opinions as to where the canal should be cut. Those that favoured the policies of Bentley, the company chairman, won the day, but it created a bitter divide which was to have repercussions for years to come.

A dispute also arose over the location of the canal terminus in Birmingham and eventually two were built: the Newhall Branch (1772) and the Paradise Street Branch (1773). The BCN had temporary offices in Newhall Street but made the Paradise Street Wharf their headquarters when these wharves were finished. The canal passed through fields right up to the outskirts of the town. Some of the less important thoroughfares crossed by swivel bridges, instead of the traditional brick, humped-back version, and the towpath was separated from the fields by a quick hedge. Paradise Street Wharf, named because it faced Paradise Street, comprised two long basins arranged side by side in the shape of a tuning fork. Here the coal boats unloaded their coal for stacking alongside the wharf. The merchants trading in coal loaded their carts to take into the town.

During these early days the BCN had its own boats for bringing coal from the mines into Birmingham, but also faced competition from private traders. Within a few years the canal company had given up the carrying trade and left the business of bringing coal into Birmingham to the traders. Wharf space became more in demand, and new wharves were established alongside the Newhall Branch. Although coal remained the principal cargo, the carriage of limestone, iron, paper and other general merchandise started to become more common. Most trade remained local and the number of boats which ventured up and down the locks between Wolverhampton and Aldersley was smaller than that which passed from Bilston to Birmingham.

The BCN proprietors faced and sometimes fought off competition from rival canal schemes which threatened their trade. In 1781 a serious threat was presented by the Birmingham & Fazeley Canal Company who proposed a new line of canal from Fazeley to the collieries around Darlaston and Wednesbury which were not adequately served by the existing canal. The BCN offered an alternative proposal, but Parliament finally sanctioned a modified Birmingham & Fazeley Canal plan two years later. A new line of canal from Fazeley to join the Newhall Branch at Farmer's Bridge and a separate section from the Wednesbury Canal at Ryders Green to Broadwaters were authorised by the Act of 1783. Within another year (1784) the two Birmingham canal companies had merged. Construction started soon after the merger. The main line of the Birmingham & Fazeley Canal extended from Birmingham and through Aston, Erdington and Coleshill to join the Coventry Canal at Fazeley. This canal, unlike the old Birmingham Canal, followed a much straighter course. More engineering was involved which included embankment and cuttings. There were two major flights of locks within the Birmingham area; the first set of locks, which became known as the Farmer's Bridge Flight, comprised thirteen locks and descended 83ft from the Birmingham (453ft) Level down to the Hospital Pond Level at Snow Hill Bridge. This canal, which is still known as the Birmingham & Fazeley, then continued to Aston where another flight of eleven locks brought the canal down to the Erdington (302ft) Level at Salford Bridge.

The canal from Farmer's Bridge through Aston to Fazeley was officially opened in 1789. But there were some problems with the construction works and commercial traffic did not properly start until a year later. At Aston a branch was made down to Digbeth, which also opened in about 1790. The Digbeth Branch descended through six locks at Ashted to a terminal basin which faced Bordesley Street.

The completion of the Fazeley route was accompanied by the lowering of the locks at Smethwick. It had been a burden to the boatmen who had to endure six locks on the climb from Birmingham and at least another three down again to get over the Smethwick Summit. Between 1789 and 1790 the top three locks either side of the summit were removed and the bottom three on the Smethwick side doubled to aid navigation. Both sets of improvements encouraged commercial canal carrying through Birmingham and a number of canal-carrying firms started to regularly pass through the town; carriers' wharves were established at Aston Junction, Broad Street and the Crescent.

The year 1799 saw the completion of the Warwick & Birmingham Canal between Digbeth and Budbrooke, while from 1795 the Worcester & Birmingham Canal had been gradually extended through Selly Oak, Kings Norton and Tardebigge to reach the River Severn at Diglis in 1815. Each of these two waterways, in turn, had links with other canals, which added to the complex network of waterways through which Birmingham was becoming a natural centre of trade. Meanwhile, the BCN had continued to expand in size, adding extra mileage to Walsall (1799) and linking Toll End with Tipton (1809). Some minor improvements had also been carried out near Birmingham where some of the tight turns had been altered and widened.

Minor improvements continued to be made to the Birmingham Canal up to 1820, but after this date a programme of sustained alterations were commenced that were to extend the system further. The Birmingham Canal Navigations Company engaged Thomas Telford to assist them in the new work. Telford was already an eminent engineer and had planned roads and canals throughout the country. He is perhaps best remembered for engineering new canals and roads in Shropshire and Scotland. On the Birmingham Canal Telford's major work was the New Main Line between Birmingham and Wolverhampton. Thomas Telford came to the Birmingham Canal in 1824 and spent a few days riding on horseback around the area before formulating his plans. He found a narrow waterway clogged with boats. It was a canal where boatmen fought each other to get to the locks or for right of passage in a restricted channel. Telford resolved to remedy the problem by building a wide waterway with a double towpath. These were the days of horse boats where every movement on the waterway was done either with a horse, by bow hauling or by poling.

Telford's scheme enabled traffic to flow easily, without boat lines getting entangled leading to the inevitable arguments. Telford's improvements are visible today on the section that extends through Smethwick and beyond to Coseley. The double towpath main line starts from Broad Street and passes through Ladywood and Winson Green to Smethwick and the deep cutting beyond. The new line continues through Albion and Tipton, maintaining the same level of 453ft (or Birmingham Level) throughout before reaching the three Factory locks which take the boats up to, or down from, the 473ft (or Wolverhampton) Level. The work through Smethwick was completed in 1829. In addition to the new wide waterway, modifications were made to the water supply that included a new reservoir at Edgbaston and two canal feeders: one feeder brought water from Titford Pools and the other united the reservoir with the Engine Arm at Smethwick. Most of Brindley's old canal was retained and now formed loops and branches off the New Main Line. Industry flourished on these backwater branches, which contributed to the trade on these local canals.

The BCN continued to expand, merging with the Wyrley & Essington Canal in 1840 and Dudley Canal in 1846. They also continued to build new lines such as the Tame Valley Canal (1844), which linked Salford on the Birmingham & Fazeley with the Walsall Canal near Ocker Hill. Surprisingly, more additional mileage was added to BCN between 1840 and 1860 than had been in all the previous years and in spite of growing competition from railways. Part of the expansion was due to the trade connected with the local iron industry, which was at its peak between 1850 and 1870. Coal traffic also continued to increase; even though Black Country coal mining was on the decline by this time, the development of the Cannock Chase Coalfield during the 1860s more than compensated for the loss. Developments in technology led to new business ventures seeking canal-side locations where coal continued to be delivered cheaply. A new trade was also created in association with the railway carriers.

The Birmingham Canal Navigations Company had actively promoted a new railway from Birmingham to Wolverhampton through joining in partnership with railway operators. It was a partnership which eventually led to railway control, but the amount of canal-side industry was such that a trade was established where goods passed between railway interchange basins and works on the canal.

Trade flourished on the Birmingham Canal up to around 1914, when a slow and steady decline set in. There was also a change in how boats were worked. From 1912 a number of motorboats started to appear, driven by petrol or paraffin. Commercial carriers such as Fellows, Morton & Clayton started to change over their fleets to motorboat operation and the days of the horse boat were numbered on the long-distance trade. On the northern BCN some coal carriers started to use tugs on the long lockless sections from the Cannock Chase Coalfield. Loading times for coal boats could be lengthy, which led to delays in coal delivery. The process was speeded up through the use of tugs, which ferried empty boats to the collieries and collected loaded boats without having to wait to be loaded.

During the First World War canals and railways were controlled and subsidised by the government. For railway-controlled canals this control came into effect almost from the start of the war, but for other waterways, and some commercial operators, control and subsidy did not take effect until 1917. Government control continued until 1920, when the canals and canal carriers were left again to fend for themselves. In the intervening time costs had risen and canal boat operation was becoming less and less competitive.

Coal remained the largest single commodity carried on the BCN, but there was a whole host of other cargoes. Commercial carriers' depots were crammed with every conceivable commodity from metal goods to tea. Private boats also handled a variety of goods, which included bricks, chemicals, cement, foundry sand and stone. Birmingham Corporation was an important canal user. The electricity, gas, public works and salvage depots all generated canal trade. Passenger boats have had mixed success. Better known as packet boats, these vessels carried passengers along the Old, and later New, Main Lines calling at strategic points to pick up and set down. Packet boats have been recorded operating on the Birmingham Canal as early as 1800, but the service had all but ceased by 1852. During April 1919, however, Dunlop Ltd commenced a passenger boat service along the Birmingham & Fazeley Canal from Aston to their Erdington works. Each boat could take 100 people at a time. It was at its busiest in 1920, when the boats carried 5,000 workers a week, but stopped after a new tram route was opened to Fort Dunlop.

The local canal trade commonly used the day boat, which was an open boat often lacking the basic comforts of a cabin. They moved all sorts of bulk material from coal to night soil. Major canal closures commenced during the 1950s, but most of the network within the

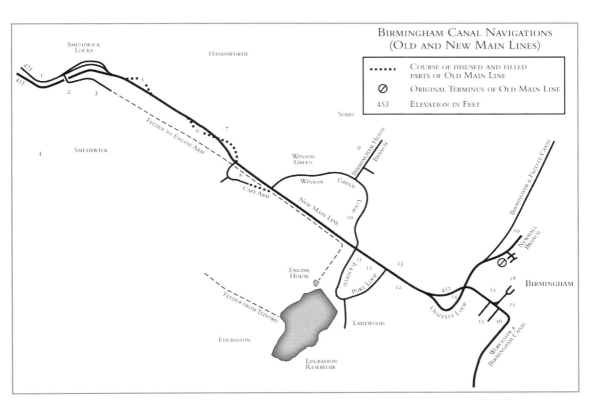

Birmingham Old & New Main Lines

1	Brasshouse Lane Engine House	13	Monument Lane Railway interchange basin
2	Engine Arm Aqueduct		
3	Bridge Street Engine Houses	14	Stewarts & Lloyds Tube Works, Nile Street
4	Site of Great Smethwick Reservoirs		
5	Tangyes Works	15	Warehouses & Wharves
6	Muntz's French Wall Works/Bordesley Steel & Ironworks	16	Gas Street Gasworks
		17	Eyre Street Wharves (Ironworks & Varnish)
7	Boulton & Watt, Soho Foundry		
8	GKN Heath Street Works	18	Paradise Street Wharves
9	Soho Glassworks	19	Newhall Street Wharves (Newhall Ring)
10	Thomas Piggott, Bridge & Gasholder Factory		
11	Docker Brothers Paint Factory	xxx	Course of filled-in parts of Old Main Line
12	Belliss & Morcom Marine Engine Factory, Rotton Park & Ledsam Street	Y	Original terminus of Old Main Line

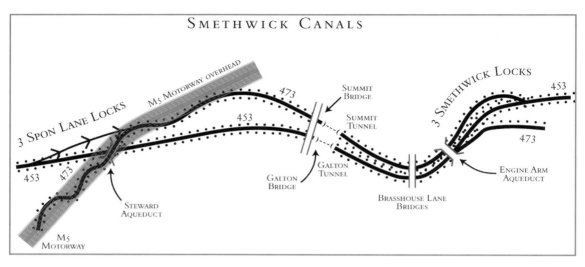

Modern map of the canal arrangement at Smethwick.

City of Birmingham remained intact, although less used. Commercial traffic had virtually ceased by 1965, although the odd boat still continued to come through, and still does. Several factors had influenced this state of affairs. The significant increase in road haulage companies had eroded the remaining canal trade and closures had decimated the local colliery industry. British Railways had from 1954 decided to withdraw its own boatage services and interchange basins were shut down. Closures had also affected other canal-side industries. Many gasworks ceased production during the 1960s to make way for the new natural gas, and the smaller coal-fired power stations stopped generating electricity as the Central Electricity Generating Board rationalised its industry. But the most serious effect on trade had been the severe winter of 1963. Thick ice had prevented passage along the waterways for months. Many of the smaller traders were consequently forced off the canals and out of business. Traffic on the Birmingham waterways today is generally restricted to the boaters and the hire-boaters, whose gaily painted craft regularly line the towpaths. The canal side, which for many years was shut off behind grimy old buildings, has been opened up. New residential, hotel and recreational buildings have sprung up alongside the waterway.

The canal around Broad Street had seen particular change. Once it was hidden behind brick walls, factories and warehouses; now the factories have been demolished and the cottages and warehouses have been converted into coffee houses, pubs and restaurants. Trip boats take people around the local waterways and most towpaths are open to the public to walk around as they will. The International Convention Centre, the National Indoor Arena and the Sea Life Centre have frontages to the canal here. During the 1990s a new business centre opened at Brindley Place and the Crescent Theatre relocated to a canal-side location on the Oozells Loop. Planners have carefully blended the old with the new. Austin Court is now a conference centre, but started life in the early 1800s as a nail warehouse. Residential properties have also come to the canal side, reversing a trend of moving people out of the eighteenth- and nineteenth-century courts and alleyways and into the modern version of apartments.

In Sherborne Street the Fellows, Morton & Clayton warehouse was converted into apartments for residential use. Similar scenes are emerging along the waterway from Salford Bridge to Summer Lane and Aston to Digbeth. The provision of mixed-use residential and leisure facilities still continues as developers cast their net in an ever-increasing circle. Yet not every change has received general approval. It is a continually changing scene.

The Birmingham Canal in Birmingham has an extensive mileage. Parts of the Old and New Main Lines, the Newhall Branch, the Birmingham & Fazeley Canal and the Tame Valley Canal are all situated within the boundaries of Greater Birmingham. We begin our study with the New Main Line.

Paradise Street, or Old Wharf, was the terminus of the BCN from 1773. At the front of the wharf, facing Paradise Street, the canal company erected offices. It was a distinctive design, comprising an octagonal central building with two wings – one either side of separate entrances on to the wharf. (*Birmingham Reference Library*)

The Paradise Street offices were the headquarters for the BCN. It was here that they decided policy and conducted the day-to-day running of the company. It was from the steps that led up to the entrance, fronted by iron railings, that John Wesley preached on one of his visits to Birmingham. The Paradise Street offices were demolished in 1912 when the company headquarters moved to new office accommodation a short distance away in Daimler House, Paradise Street. (*Birmingham Reference Library*)

Bridge Street Bridge, Old Wharf. The entrance to Old Wharf was through the brick bridge under Bridge Street. The towpath was not carried through the bridge hole, which meant that all unpowered boats had to be poled through. It is not clear whether the passage on the right is the towing pathway or a vault. The building above the bridge is part of the Cement Wharf used by Greaves, Bull & Lakin. (*Birmingham Reference Library*)

Old Wharf. The Old Wharf, Paradise Street, was essentially a collection of coal merchants' wharves. Each merchant had a designated wharf space where the coal was stacked and graded before sale. In later years, Old Wharf was home to a number of canal carriers who specialised in the coal trade. When the Paradise Street offices were closed and demolished in 1912, the main entrance to the wharf was moved to Bridge Street. The last trade directory entry for Old Wharf was published in 1927 when a handful of carriers and merchants remained. This picture was taken after closure and before the wharf was filled in. From 1773 until 1927 Old Wharf had been busy with carts and horses. Generations of families had worked on this wharf, son following father into the coal trade. The line of offices that forms the perimeter of the wharf with Paradise Street was constructed on the site of the old canal offices. (*Birmingham Reference Library*)

Gas Street Basin, 1913. The scene on the opposite side of Bridge Street looking across what is now called Gas Street Basin. The photographer is standing on the towpath in front of the canal cottage which is now part of the Tap & Spile public house. On the left is the towpath side bridge over Broad Street Basin, while on the right is the cement wharf and one end of the Worcester Wharf warehouses. The boats are moored up against the Worcester Bar. (*Birmingham Reference Library*)

Gas Street Basin, July 1955. A horse-drawn T. & S. Element's coal boat is seen passing through Broad Street Tunnel towards the stop lock on Worcester Bar. Element's were among the last commercial carriers on the local canals and are still in business as road hauliers. (*J.G. Parkinson, courtesy of Mrs J. Parkinson*)

Gas Street Basin, 1982. The view from Bridge Street towards Gas Street is shown before Gas Street Basin was improved. Towering above the basin are two office blocks. The sixteen-floor building with the 'To Let' sign became a major office for British Rail (Rail House). This building stands on part of the old wharves that extended from Gas Street to Granville Street. Rail House had been a divisional headquarters for British Rail, was later used by Regional Railways and more recently GTRM. It was then known as Quayside Tower. Since the privatisation of the rail industry, the offices were disposed of. (*Author's collection*)

View from Broad Street Tunnel to Worcester Bar, 1982. From right to left the buildings comprise a grain warehouse, two cottages, the Birmingham Canal lock cottage, the Worcester & Birmingham toll cottage and the Worcester & Birmingham Canal Company offices. The *Ash* belonged to a fleet of narrowboats owned by the Birmingham & Midland Canal Carrying Company, which operated trip and camping boats but still did some commercial carrying. (*Author's collection*)

The Brasshouse, Broad Street, *c.* 1800. The turnpike road from Birmingham to Blakedown via Halesowen crossed the Paradise Street branch of the Birmingham at Islington (later Broad Street) Bridge. A brass works was erected nearby on the high ground above the canal. The owners were a group of businessmen known as the Birmingham Brass Company (established in 1780). Brass working was then an important local trade, but the component metals that make up brass (copper and zinc) were not obtained locally. The canal enabled the owners to transport copper and zinc oxide (calamine) to the brass works to make brass more cheaply than elsewhere. Coal needed for the furnaces was also delivered by the boatload. The brass works extended along the canal, almost to Old Turn Junction. Here, three of the distinctive furnace buildings can be seen. The fumes rise to the sky through the square openings at the top. This type of brass making changed when the process of mixing copper with spelter (metallic zinc) was developed. From 1831 the Brasshouse became a general metal warehouse. Although the furnace buildings were demolished then, the building which faced Broad Street remained; it was later used as Water Company offices and is now a pub. (*Author's collection*)

A working boat and the International Convention Centre (ICC), 1991. This winter scene shows a working boat heading off from Gas Street Basin, which has been a home to many traditional craft over the years. The canal here had been in a deep cutting with tall brick walls on either side, but the redevelopment of the area was to remove most of the evidence of this. The building of the ICC started the process when the wall and abutments that formerly supported St Peter's Place were removed. This is an early and unobstructed view of the ICC. In 1994 a footbridge was constructed across the canal to link Waters Edge and Brindley Place with the ICC, changing the view forever. The sharp-eyed might also note that the side entrance to The Crown (now Edwards) had not yet been made, and the shops over the canal on Broad Street still have the names of the owners. (*Author's collection*)

Old Turn Junction or Deep Cutting Junction, 1909. Wherever there was a canal crossroads on the BCN two names were commonly assigned to the one junction, and the naming depended on the direction of travel. Matters have been simplified since then and the junction is now solely called Old Turn. This view shows an empty horse-worked working boat coming from the Deep Cutting and heading towards Ladywood. The horse is out of sight, but the mast to which the rope is attached can be seen towards the front of the boat. The side bridge on the left of the picture spans Brewery Basin, and alongside are the malthouses and brewery buildings that belonged to the Birmingham Brewery. (*Birmingham Reference Library*)

Above: Old Turn Junction to Broad Street along the Deep Cutting, 1950s. The malthouses and Brewmaster's House still survive, although the Birmingham Brewery had long closed. A new feature is the traffic island and signpost. This circular island was added following discussions between the Canal Company and the LMS Railway in 1939, where fears that bombing could cause a breach down into the railway tunnel which passed underneath. The island had grooves to fix stop planks and so close off the waterway. The telegraph poles present in the previous 1909 view are absent from this one. (*Birmingham Reference Library*)

Opposite top: *President*. This 1980s view, and the subsequent two pictures, show the canal at Old Turn Junction before redevelopment transformed the area. They all show the steamer *President* as it headed towards Gas Street Basin. In this picture the steamboat is reversing back to Old Turn Junction. *President* had been down Farmer's Bridge Locks to the lock above Newhall Street, where it had been on show to members of the public attending the once-regular May traction engine rally. The view here today is completely different. On the left now stands the Malthouse public house, while on the right the ash towpath is now brick-paved and there are steps which lead up to the National Indoor Arena (NIA). (*Author's collection*)

Opposite bottom: In this second picture *President* has reversed back to the junction with the Oozells Loop. The distinctive row of curved roof structures belonged to the former Wales (Atlas) Works, which made wooden bedsteads. Their stock of wood (brought to this factory by rail and road) was stored there. (*Author's collection*)

Above: Old Turn Junction and Deep Cutting. *President* was purchased in 1973 and completely restored to its 1909 condition using a steam engine of similar construction to the original. Restoration was completed in 1978 and since then *President* has toured the canal system visiting many events and shows. Even in the year 2012 *President* continues to be a roving ambassador for the waterways. This craft represented Staffordshire in the Queen's Jubilee Pageant and steamed down the Thames with other heritage vessels. In this picture *President* is heading towards Gas Street. The Brewery Basin, the Brewmaster's House and St Peter's Place can be seen on the left, while in the centre the brick vault across the canal which supported the Church of the Messiah still remains. Tall brick walls line the towpath on both sides, rendering little access to the public and preserving the secret world that the local canals had become. (*Author's collection*)

Opposite top: Sea Life Centre. The Birmingham canal scene was transformed with the redevelopment of the old brass works and former Wales bedstead factory site. This 1997 view shows new buildings going up around Brindley Place. Construction was proceeding with No. 3 Brindley Place, while the foundations for No. 4 Brindley Place were being excavated. (*Author's collection*)

Opposite bottom: New Main Line, St Vincent Street Bridge, April 1998. A British Waterways maintenance boat approaches St Vincent Street Bridge. The row of maisonettes on the left occupy the site where the Midland Flour Mills once stood. Ahead, and through the bridge hole, is Ladywood Junction, where the Oozells Loop joins the Main Line. (*Author's collection*)

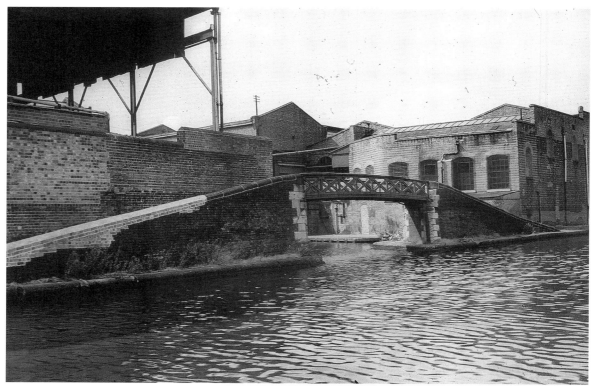

Above: Rotton Park Junction, 1966. The canal junction at Rotton Park is the only place on the BCN where two waterways cross at right angles. It is at this point that James Brindley's Old Main Line (1769) crosses Telford's New Main Line (1829). The new canal became the main artery between Birmingham and Wolverhampton, and the older line was reduced to series of loops or arms which connected with it. This view shows the bridge across the junction (Rotton Park Junction) of the Icknield Port, or Rotton Park, Loop with the main canal and is seen from under the towpath bridge that spans the other junction (Eyre Street Junction), where the Soho, or Winson Green, Loop joins the main canal. The buildings in this view include part of Docker Brothers paint factory on the left and the other buildings in Wiggin Street. (*RCHS Weaver Collection, ref. 45103*)

Opposite top: Borax Works, Ladywood. The manufacture of borax soap and soap powder was carried on by the Patent Borax Company at the Ledsam Street works from 1893. Coal and soda ash were brought by boat to these works. (*Author's collection*)

Opposite bottom: Icknield Square Junction, 1966. The Icknield Port Loop joined the New Main Line at Icknield Square Junction. Here, the Old Main Line followed the course of the loop heading up the valley to cross Edgbaston Brook and avoiding, under the James Brindley survey, the more expensive embankment across the valley. Under Thomas Telford's direction, the wide main line complete with a double towpath crossed the valley on a tall embankment to Rotton Park Junction. In later years the land enclosed by the loop was filled up with spoil and rubbish and ultimately enabled the canal company to lease sections off for industrial purposes. These leases started at Icknield Port Road and proceeded down either side of a central street (Rotton Park Street), finally reaching the New Main Line. The buildings straddling Icknield Square Junction were built for and belonged to Bellis & Morcom, marine engineers. (*RCHS Weaver Collection, ref. 45102*)

Above: Harborne Junction. When, in 1967, the railway system through Birmingham to London was converted to electric traction, first generation electric units of the class 304 type were commonly seen on local services between Birmingham and Wolverhampton. This train is seen passing the site where the Harborne Railway (1874) crossed the New Main Line at Rotton Park, 3 September 1977. (*Michael Mensing*)

Opposite top: The Skew Bridge, Dudley Road, *c.* 1913. Telford's New Main Line was cut in a straight line from Ladywood through to Winson Green with a double towpath on either side. Telford engineered two skew brick bridges across the New Main Line. This one was made to carry the Dudley Turnpike across the canal. It is still in use today, carrying the busy Dudley Road. Completed in 1828, the bridge shows little sign of wear. (*Birmingham Reference Library*)

Opposite bottom: Winson Green Toll Office. The purpose of the toll office was to ensure that the correct payment was made for each boat journey: goods carried along the canal were subject to a toll which varied according to weight and commodity. Payments were made in cash at the toll office or by account which was settled regularly. The toll keeper had to have the means of verifying boat weights, and these were usually checked by the toll office using a gauging stick against a set of graduated indexes on the boat side. The complex nature of the BCN meant that there were a number of toll offices at strategic points along the canal. Telford's New Main Line had three toll offices erected in the centre of the waterway which enabled them to gauge boats as they passed either side. These octagonal toll offices were unique to the BCN. On the other side of the office is the junction where the Soho Loop rejoins the New Main Line. (*Birmingham Reference Library*)

Above: Winson Green, 1992. All the island octagonal toll offices were removed by British Waterways after they decided to introduce a licence system, although the toll islands have remained. This view, which is taken from the feeder, shows a narrowboat passing the island on a summer afternoon. Behind the boat is the British Railways Soho Diesel and Electric Depot, which came into use as part of the electrification scheme between Birmingham and Wolverhampton (1967). What is now a heritage diesel unit can be seen on the depot. With railway privatisation Soho Depot was rebuilt as a train maintenance depot. (*Author's collection*)

Opposite: Winson Green Toll Office, changing shifts. In order to reach the toll office, staff had to cross a wooden plank which pivoted at the side of the office. Note the sign banning cycling on towpaths; today, cycling is encouraged on some towpaths, where there are designated cycleways. Behind the toll house is the embankment that carried the feeder from Edgbaston Reservoir to Smethwick. (*National Waterways Museum, Ellesmere Port*)

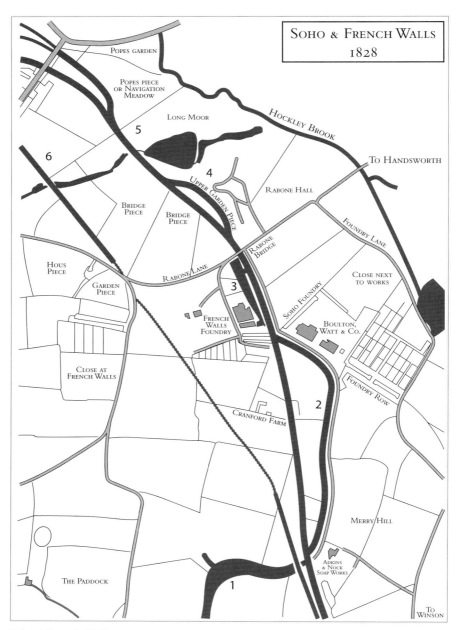

Soho & French Walls

1   Cape Arm (Brindley's Old Main Line)
2   The Old Main Line, through the Soho Foundry (now mostly filled in)
3   French Walls Foundry Basin (Old Main Line)
4   The Old Main Line at Rabone Hall (later Tangye's Works)
5   Telford's New Main Line
6   The Engine Arm Feeder from Rotton Park

Soho, 1828. This map shows the course of the Old and New Main Lines through Soho and French Walls. The Soho Foundry (Boulton & Watt) then occupied a smaller area than it does today. The nearby French Walls Foundry was previously used as a flour mill.

Soho Foundry and French Walls, 1993. A pair of working boats is seen passing the Soho Foundry. Telford engineered a wide canal through the land here, reducing the old Brindley Canal to loop and basin status. The Old Main Line passed through the Soho Foundry site and part was kept in water to serve the foundry after the Telford canal was completed. There is still a side bridge over the entrance to this basin. The original Soho Foundry was erected for Boulton & Watt in 1796 to manufacture castings for their steam engines, but was later taken over and enlarged by Avery's to manufacture weighing machines and scales. Those buildings beside the towpath were erected during the Avery era. (*Author's collection*)

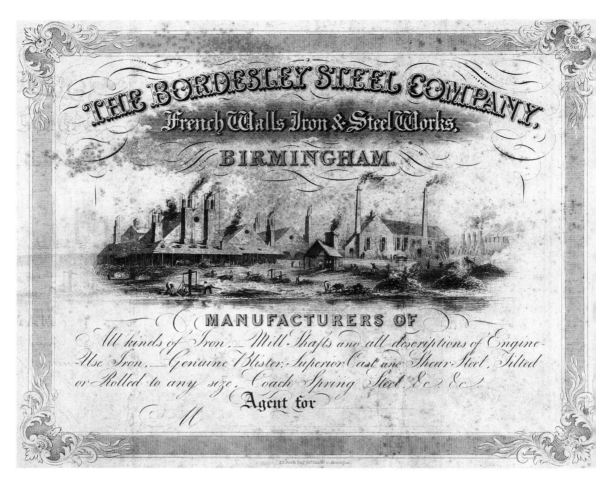

THE BORDESLEY STEEL COMPANY,
French Walls Iron & Steel Works,
BIRMINGHAM.

MANUFACTURERS OF

All kinds of Iron, Mill Shafts and all descriptions of Engine-Use Iron, Genuine Blister, Superior Cast and Shear Steel, Tilted or Rolled to any size, Coach Spring Steel &c. &c.

Agent for

Bordesley Steel Company, French Walls. Boulton & Watt owned the land on both sides of the canal. During the 1830s they converted the French Walls Foundry into an iron and steelworks which was let to the Bordesley Steel Company. Steel was then manufactured from the best-quality iron using charcoal in cementation and crucible furnaces. All raw materials would have come to the French Walls Works by boat. Steel making here was short-lived. George Muntz took over these premises in 1842 to manufacture Muntz's Metal, which was an alloy of copper and zinc used to sheave the bottom of wooden sailing ships. (*Birmingham Library Archives, Boulton & Watt Collection*)

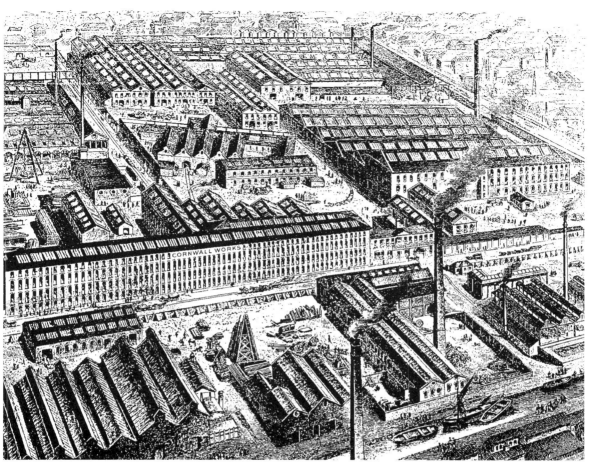

The Cornwall Works. Tangye Brothers purchased Rabone Hall in 1862 and established the Cornwall Works beside the Birmingham Canal. Here they achieved a worldwide reputation for the manufacture of pumps and lifting jacks. This engraving shows the extensive group of buildings that comprised the Cornwall Works, *c.* 1880. There has been some artistic inaccuracy on the part of the artist, including the placing of a sailing boat on the canal. (*Birmingham Reference Library*)

Above: New Main Line, Smethwick, at the junction with the Old Main Line. An enduring scene on the Birmingham Canal Navigation is the day boat, which was used to move a variety of items ranging from iron goods to rubbish and sand. Its main cargo was coal, moving it from the collieries to the Birmingham manufacturers. In this case an empty boat is being brought along the New Main Line by a horse and its driver. The person who guided the horse did so from the rear to ensure maximum control in the difficult places, such as over bridges and when passing other craft. (*RCHS Hugh Compton Collection, ref. 64222*)

Opposite top: Engine Aqueduct and Gauging Station, *c*. 1913. Thomas Telford designed an elegant iron aqueduct to bring the water from Edgbaston Reservoir across the New Main Line and into the upper Wolverhampton Level. Behind it is the Smethwick gauging (or indexing) station, which was built in the 1830s and demolished in the 1940s. Gauging stations were created to weigh boats and calibrate them with graduated indexes. As designs of boats varied, company policy was changed and from 1872 it was decided to reconstruct the Smethwick station for dry inch gauging. With this process a unique gauging table was compiled for each boat so that more accurate measurements could be made by the tolls clerks. (*Birmingham Reference Library*)

Opposite bottom: Engine Aqueduct, 1990. The aqueduct, which is now a scheduled ancient monument, carries the Engine Arm over the New Main Line. It comprises an iron trough supported on a cast-iron laced arch with brick and stone abutments. This decorative structure was repainted in 1985. (*Author's collection*)

The Spoilbank Smethwick,

Dibhtinbalets

Above: The Spoilbank, Smethwick, as seen from Brasshouse Lane. This view is reproduced from an early 1900s postcard by Nightingale, and by the name indicates former deposits of excavation spoil. It shows both the Old and New Main Lines busy with traffic. The Great Western Railway Bridge and Galton Bridge can just be made out in the distance crossing the New Main Line. The Old Main Line curves away to the right. On the far right is the engine house and stack which recirculated water between the two levels. It replaced the old Bridge Street engines in 1892. The footpath on the far right above the Old Main Line has been taken by some historians to be the route of the original 1769 canal before the summit was lowered in 1789–90. That view was challenged and it has become the belief that the original course curved across the route of the New Main Line through, or near, what is now the engine house, before swinging back on to the present course. The construction of the deep cutting for the New Main Line in 1826–29 caused a further straightening and diversion of the Old Main Line at this point. However, putting forward this interpretation for how and why the excavation of the Old and New Main Lines happened leaves a few unanswered questions, particularly with regards to how the original 1769 level was taken down 18ft. Surviving records indicate that contractors changed sides when digging down at this spot. They worked first on the south side and then transferred to the north near Roebuck Lane. For this reason, the earlier belief that the original route did follow the course of the footpath on the far right is again a valid suggestion. (*National Waterways Museum, Ellesmere Port*)

Opposite top: The 1892 Smethwick Engine House underwent extensive restoration during the 1980s. Part of the work included the construction of a new chimney stack. (*Author's collection*)

Opposite bottom: Smethwick Old and New Main Lines, the view in 1999. The restored engine house and stack are seen centre right. Gone are the telegraph poles and the canal-side cottages beside the Old Main Line, and Galton Bridge is hidden behind the road embankment and tunnel over the New Main Line. (*Author's collection*)

Galton Bridge from the towpath, *c.* 1913. Galton Bridge was completed in 1829. It is an iron bridge with brick and stone abutments, manufactured by the Horseley Company of Tipton to the designs of Thomas Telford. It has a 150ft span which carries a 30ft-wide roadway over the canal. The height from the waterline to the underside of the arch is 75ft. (*Birmingham Reference Library*)

Galton Bridge. A local London & North Western Railway (LNWR) train from Wolverhampton to Birmingham New Street approaches Smethwick. It is seen passing Galton Bridge, which carries Roebuck Lane over the New Main Line. (*London & North Western Railway Society Collection*)

Overleaf: GWR Railway Bridge. In this view from Galton Bridge a tug is about to pass under the railway bridge. This bridge carries the railway from Stourbridge to Birmingham Snow Hill, which opened in 1867. Both towpaths were in reasonable condition; since then the far towpath has deteriorated through lack of use. The most important change since this picture was taken is the construction of Galton Bridge station. Two of the station platforms are now fixed on either side of the bridge parapet. Another important observation is the depth of the cutting at this point. (*Michael Mensing*)

Oozells Street Loop looking towards Sherborne Street. The Oozells Street Loop forms part of Brindley's original canal. On the left, coal boats can be seen lined up against Oozells Street Wharf. Here, coal was graded and sized before distribution by the coal merchants. Coal wharves were a common sight on the canal, but most were not as large as Oozells Street; most, in fact, were simply a couple of boat lengths. These wharves, like their railway station counterpart, supplied the domestic and industrial market. On the right is the Albion Tube Works, Nile Street, then part of the Stewarts & Lloyds group. Coal boats are also lined up alongside the Tube Works Wharf. Lap-welded iron tubes were manufactured here for boilers and the gas and water industry. In addition to coal, metal strip would have been brought here by boat to be made into tubes. (*Birmingham Reference Library*)

Sherborne Street Wharf, *c.* 1947. This view shows a Fellows, Morton & Clayton butty, *Madeley* (1928), tied up alongside the wharf. Sherborne Street Wharf was originally much smaller, but was enlarged by Fellows, Morton & Clayton during 1938 when they constructed a new warehouse on adjacent land. Birmingham Corporation had plans to redevelop the Crescent Wharves, and Fellows, Morton & Clayton – fearing the loss of their wharf there – moved this part of their operation to Sherborne Street. It was the last new canal warehouse to be constructed in central Birmingham. Fellows, Morton & Clayton went into voluntary liquidation in 1949: their premises and boats passed to the Docks & Inland Waterways Executive. Sherborne Street remained a busy wharf handling chiefly metal goods brought in by boat. In 1956 Sherborne Street Wharf belonged to the British Transport Commission, and functioned as part of the British Transport Waterways organisation. (*Birmingham Archives, Fellows, Morton & Clayton MS*)

Above: Sherborne Street Wharf, 1996. There was a canal arm which came off the Oozells Street Loop and extended beyond Sherborne Street. Only part of the arm is still in water, and this came to be used by the hire and trip boat company as a boat dock. Originally Sherborne Street Wharf was continued along this arm, and there was also wharf space for Baldwin's Paper Mills and the Rowley Regis Granite Company on the opposite side. Baldwin's & Co. transferred their paper-making business to Kings Norton, but retained the original mill as a warehouse. (*Author's collection*)

Opposite top: St Vincent Street Bridge and Ladywood Junction. Before the drastic changes made to this spot in the last ten years, there were a number of old factory buildings still extant that lined the old route of the Oozells Loop. One of these buildings had once been used to make and assemble Quadrant bicycles. The old towpath that extended as far as Sherborne Street Bridge can be seen on the right by the boats. Access by this time had been restricted to those who moored boats there. (*Author's collection*)

Opposite bottom: Icknield Port Loop, 1997. The Sherborne Wharf trip boat *Jericho* is seen passing along the Sherborne Loop towards the junction with the New Main Line. There are parts on both the Oozells Loop and the Icknield Port Loop where the towpath is not accessible to walkers. In this view the towpath, which is on the right, terminates by the brick wall. (*Author's collection*)

Above: Oozells Loop and Fellows, Morton & Clayton Works. This 1990s view looks along Oozells Street Loop from Ladywood Junction back towards the Sherborne Street warehouse. After several years of dereliction, the Fellows, Morton & Clayton warehouse, of 1938, was converted into apartments for residential use. The essential shape and fabric was retained, although the hoists and canopy over the waterway have been removed. Prior to 1938 the view from this point would have been very different. From the early 1800s the Old Union Mill was a dominant feature on the skyline. (*Author's collection*)

Opposite top: Oozells Loop, 2002. An important transformation during the lead-up to the millennium was the completion of the Brindley Place development. With Brindley Place on the left and Symphony Court on the right, this view is very different from the coal wharves and tube works that were canal-side features 100 years earlier. The architect who designed the modern buildings in Brindley Place has incorporated a feature that resembles the former Wales Timber Wharf sheds. (*Author's collection*)

Opposite bottom: Birmingham Heath Branch, as seen from Lodge Road, 1982. The Birmingham Heath Branch was constructed from the Soho Loop to Soho Wharf, a terminal basin near Matthew Boulton's Soho Manufactory. The top part of the branch was severed when the Great Western Railway widened its line from Hockley to Handsworth. The branch then terminated at a wharf on the east side of Lodge Road. On the left are the former Hockley railway interchange basins. In the centre is the side bridge over the entrance to the branch and on the right is the boundary wall for part of the All Saints' Hospital site. These basins were redeveloped by British Waterways as Hockley Port for boaters' residential moorings and are still maintained as such by the Canal & River Trust. (*Author's collection*)

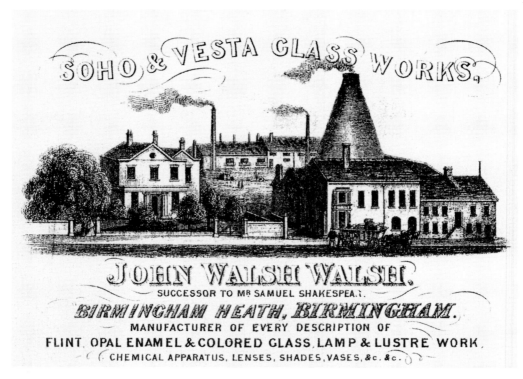

Above: The Soho & Vesta Glassworks, Birmingham Heath Branch, Lodge Road. Samuel Shakespear established the Soho Flint Glassworks beside the Birmingham Heath Branch with a frontage to Lodge Road. There was a group of glassworks around Birmingham which relied on transport by canal. Soho Glassworks was the last to close. The cone was a skyline feature until the 1940s. The cone base was recently uncovered to record the remains before the site was cleared for new houses. (*Author's collection*)

Opposite top: Coal Wharf and Timber Yard, Birmingham Heath Branch. The Birmingham Heath Branch terminated at a wharf near Soho Pool. When the Great Western Railway widened their railway and removed a tunnel under this branch, the waterway was shortened to a wharf beside Lodge Road (and the Soho Glassworks) and a timber yard. (*Author's collection*)

Opposite bottom: Regents Grove Ironworks, Cape Arm, 1872. The Cape Arm was originally part of Brindley's Old Main Line, but was reduced to branch status when Telford's New Main Line was completed to Smethwick. The canal was lined by factories and works on both sides: these included Bolt, Nut and Screw Works which became part of the vast Guest, Keen and Nettlefold empire (GKN). There were several ironworks that worked pig iron up in wrought-iron products. For a brief time there was a blast furnace at the Cape, which was the closest canal-served blast furnace to Birmingham. The entrance to the arm passed through a short tunnel under the Engine Arm feeder and part of this canal remains in water surrounded by buildings and factories in mixed occupancy since the closure of the GKN works. There are plans to redevelop this whole site as a new Sandwell Hospital. (*Author's collection*)

REGENT GROVE IRON WORKS, CAPE, BIRMINGHAM.

Cape Arm, 2012. Despite a lengthy period of disuse, parts of the canal remain in water surrounded by old factories and demolished buildings. It is one of the most secret parts of the Birmingham Canal Navigation, especially when it is recalled that the waterway in the foreground was part of the main line until 1829. (*Author's collection*)

The Soho Loop, 1920s. This aerial view of the waterway shows the crossing of the Old and New Main Lines at Rotton Park Junction. The Soho Loop (Old Main Line) is the canal on the right of the picture. There are a number of canal-side factories, centre left, which front Heath Street, where boats are moored alongside. It was a common feature along the Birmingham canals for boats to tie up, load and unload through door spaces in the side of the building. Sometimes a canopy was provided overhead to give a measure of protection from the rain. The towpath follows the right-hand bank of the Soho Loop. Next to it is Eyre Street Basin, which runs parallel to the loop. It was separated from the towpath by a tall brick wall. The LNWR follows the New Main Line from Birmingham to Wolverhampton. A Precursor tank engine can be seen on the railway travelling light engine back to Birmingham. There is also a small saddle-tank shunting engine at the head of a train of four wagons in front of the carriage shed. (*Aerofilms Ltd*)

Above: Smethwick Junction from the Old Main Line, *c.* 1913. Two Horseley Company roving bridges can be seen, which were put into place when Telford's New Main Line was constructed. These bridges enabled the boat horses to cross over from one towpath to the other. The boat in the distance is following Telford's New Main Line northwards. (*Birmingham Reference Library*)

Opposite top: Smethwick Power Station, 1905. Rabone Lane Power Station was commissioned in 1905. It was constructed to supply direct current to the Birmingham & Midland Tramways, which operated the electric tramways between Birmingham, Smethwick and Dudley, but also provided electricity for lighting and local industry. This station was purchased by the Shropshire, Staffordshire & Worcestershire Electric Power Company in 1908, which added extra plant and subsequently enlarged the power station. (*Author's collection*)

Opposite bottom: Smethwick Locks, 1913. The photographer is standing on the side bridge that crosses the Engine Arm, and is looking towards the top pair of locks at Smethwick. A number of boats loaded with coal are moored on the left, waiting to discharge their cargoes at the basin belonging to the Smethwick Ironworks (Manchester Works). The buildings on the right include a canal house and toll office. (*Birmingham Reference Library*)

Above: Evered Works, Smethwick Locks, 1996. Evered & Co. established the Surrey Works beside the locks at Smethwick to make gas fittings and ornamental work, such as brass chandeliers. Their premises extended along the old line of locks, now filled in. The name 'Evered', which appears on the side of the building, was visible to generations of boat people who passed this way. (*Author's collection*)

Opposite top: Smethwick Locks, 2011. Narrowboats are lined up to descend Smethwick Locks after the Birmingham Canal Navigations Society Bonfire Rally. A replica toll office was built for British Waterways to commemorate those demolished. When this picture was taken, the structure had been recently restored after vandalism. (*Author's collection*)

Opposite bottom: Smethwick Locks and Factories, 1920s. Here can be seen a number of canal-side works and the line of the old and new lock flight at Smethwick. On the extreme left of the picture are the canal cottages, toll house and the roof of the gauging station. The Engine Aqueduct and the Smethwick Salvage Depot (top left) are also visible. The Smethwick Ironworks, Doulton's Pottery and the District Iron & Steel Works occupy much of the centre of the picture. The District Iron & Steel Works (top right) was rebuilt during the 1930s. This view shows many of the original buildings that were later replaced. (*Aerofilms Ltd*)

Above: Engine Arm, October 1998. The Engine Arm is the navigable part of the feeder from Edgbaston Reservoir completed between 1828 and 1829. The navigation enabled coal boats to get up to the canal pumping engines in Bridge Street, but came to be used for commercial purposes when a number of works and factories were established alongside its banks. The quiet waters of the Engine Arm still see the occasional boat: keen boaters often make the trip up the arm as part of the Inland Waterways Association BCN Challenge, and there is a boat gathering for the Birmingham Canal Navigations Society Bonfire Rally on the first Saturday in November. The person with the strimmer was cutting the grass ready for the next Bonfire Rally. (*Author's collection*)

Opposite top: Smethwick Pumping Engine, Bridge Street. The Bridge Street pumping engine was designed and constructed by Boulton & Watt and commenced work here during July 1779. This engine, and another of 1804, assisted the recirculation of water between the Birmingham and Wolverhampton Level until 1892, when they were replaced by the Brasshouse Lane engines. The photograph, taken in 1897, shows the 1779 engine house brickwork being taken down prior to moving the engine to Ocker Hill. The engine house behind the 1779 building held the Boulton & Watt engine of 1804. After a period of 'preservation' at Ocker Hill, the 1779 engine went to the Birmingham Museum of Science and Industry where it eventually became a working exhibit there. With the closure of this museum, which was regretted by some, the engine was moved again and is now on display at Millennium Point. (*Author's collection*)

Opposite bottom: Old and New Main Line, Smethwick, 1980s. This shot was taken from the Steps, which is a footbridge that crosses the railway and road. Both Old (left) and New (right) Main Lines are visible from this spot; Brasshouse Lane is in the foreground. The District Iron & Steel Works comes down to the edge of the Old Main Line on the left, while the factories that line Rolfe Street are on the right. A solitary telegraph pole also stands on the right: the group at Smethwick had to be especially tall to take the wires over Brasshouse Lane Bridge. The name 'Brasshouse' is derived from the brass house that was originally on the District Works site. When the canal was first opened to this point in 1769 there were another three locks before the summit. The first of these three would have been centre left, and the whole of the deep cutting on the right was then at the normal ground level. (*Author's collection*)

Roebuck Lane Bridge, Old Main Line, *c.* 1930. This motorboat could be in the heart of the country instead of the industrial Black Country. Roebuck Lane Bridge was completed in 1790 and still carries the date plate. It replaced an earlier bridge which had existed before the summit was lowered from 491ft to 473ft between 1789 and 1790. The sheer height of the brickwork meant its construction was in itself an important engineering feat. The original route is believed to have been on the far left where navvies would have laboured, digging out the spoil and barrowing it on to spoil banks or into the holds of boats. In order to speed up the process, the canal company financed the hire of gins and horses to assist the removal of earth from the deep cutting. The view is different now as a road runs parallel to Roebuck Lane at this point. The canal today passes underneath through a concrete-lined tunnel. (*Sandwell Libraries*)

Roebuck Lane Bridge, *c.* 1913. This view is taken from the towpath looking through the arches of Roebuck Lane Bridge and the Great Western Railway Bridge. The boats seen moored on the right have been loaded with coal from the Sandwell Park Colliery Wharf and loading chutes, which can be seen beyond the bridges. Coal was brought down to this wharf from the Sandwell Park and Jubilee Collieries. (*Birmingham Reference Library*)

The canal cottages at Farmer's Bridge and Kingston Row, 1985. This view, looking from Tindal Bridge, has changed since the picture was taken. When the Newhall Branch was completed to this point in 1769 there was an accommodation bridge over the canal which crossed where the first boat is moored. The landowner was James Farmer, a Birmingham gunmaker, and the bridge became known as Farmer's Bridge. The bridge was taken down when canal widening was carried out during the 1820s and road traffic was diverted to Tindal Bridge. The approach to Farmer's Bridge on the right became part of Kingston Row, and there are still a number of fine Georgian brick cottages here. (*Author's collection*)

Farmer's Bridge Junction, *c.* 1913. Canal boats were constructed in all shapes and sizes, but their basic dimensions were dictated by the locks they passed through. Boats that navigated the Birmingham Canal Navigations were usually from 69ft to 71ft long and 6ft 10in wide. Those engaged in the carrying trade could have one or two cabins, but most were simply open and used to carry items such as coal relatively short distances. In this photograph a carrier's boat is seen coming out of the top lock. This vessel has a small front cabin in addition to the usual back cabin; the boat next to it has only the one cabin. The Newhall Branch can be seen on the right, while the Crescent Wharf warehouses line the waterway on the far right. Crescent Wharf was an important carriers' depot and a number of independent canal carrying companies had wharves here: firms such as George Ryder Bird, John Whitehouse & Son, German Wheatcroft and Crowley & Co. They gave way to the Shropshire Union Carrying Company (SUCC), which by 1900 occupied about two-thirds of the warehouses. (*Birmingham Reference Library*)

Cambrian Wharf, *c.* 1913. A part of the Crescent Wharf nearest Farmer's Bridge Junction became known as Cambrian Wharf. There were limestone and cement wharves and a warehouse used by the Oldbury brewer Walter Showell, who brought his ale in by boat. Three narrowboats, *Lorna*, *Elizabeth* and *Four Sisters*, are seen moored up alongside the towpath. *Lorna* belonged to the Shropshire Union Carrying Company, which had warehouses on the Crescent. All three are typical craft from the horse boat days. (*Birmingham Reference Library*)

Birmingham & Fazeley Canal, Cambrian Wharf, February 1994. This view looks along the former Newhall Branch towards the junction with the Birmingham & Fazeley Canal at Farmer's Bridge. It is a scene that has changed almost completely from the days when the waterway was busy with boats waiting their turn to load or unload at the Crescent Wharves. New buildings, including the NIA, dominate the skyline. The only survivor from the past is the white-painted canal cottage in the centre of the picture. A couple of working boats can be seen in this shot. One is the *Mountbatten* (centre right): this is an Admiral-class motorboat built for British Waterways by Yarwoods of Northwich in 1958. It is one of the few working boats on the canal that is still seen, supplying coal to the boat owner. (*Author's collection*)

Fellows, Morton & Clayton Warehouse, Crescent Wharf, *c.* 1930. The Shropshire Union Carrying Company was a subsidiary of the LNWR Company. The SUCC empire was broken up and disposed of in 1922, prior to the formation of the London, Midland & Scottish Railway. The Crescent Warehouses were taken over by Fellows, Morton & Clayton who continued to use the buildings for canal transport. The SUCC had made many improvements and alterations which Fellows, Morton & Clayton inherited. In this view a boat on the Newhall Branch is being unloaded by a hoist. (*Birmingham Archives, Fellows, Morton & Clayton MS*)

Above: Fellows, Morton & Clayton steam lorry, *c.* 1930. Most canal carriers had a fleet of road vehicles for transporting goods around the towns they served, and sometimes long distance when the canals were frozen. Horse-drawn carts and ingots were common, but in this picture a Foden steam lorry is seen at the back of the Crescent Wharf loading copper ingots previously delivered by boat. (*Birmingham Archives, Fellows, Morton & Clayton MS*)

Opposite: Fellows, Morton & Clayton, Crescent Wharf, *c.* 1930. Part of the Crescent Wharf extended on to and along the Gibson's Arm towards Cambridge Street. Here, the view is from a part of the ex-SUCC warehouse with a wharf alongside the Gibson's Arm. Metal bars are being unloaded. (*Birmingham Archives, Fellows, Morton & Clayton MS*)

Above: Gibson's Lock, *c.* 1930. The private Gibson's Branch passed under Cambridge Street and through one lock to reach the Gibson & Baskerville Basins. Water was raised into the basins by a steam engine beside the lock. Gibson's Arm served a number of factories including those belonging to R.W. Winfield Brass Bedstead and Chandelier Works, and Thomas Bolton's Wire and Cable Works. The depth of the lock has never been fully determined, although the land levels would suggest the rise was about 8ft. One of the two basins was filled in when the Hall of Memory was built; the rest survived until 1938. (*Birmingham Archives, Fellows, Morton & Clayton MS*)

Opposite: Newhall Branch canal breach, 1901. These two photographs show a Worsey & Co. coal boat which had broken its back when drawn through the breach near the end of the canal. George Jones Iron Founders had been making improvements to their foundry, but workmen had worked too close to the basin. A breach occurred and the water flooded down Newhall Street, causing extensive damage. (*Birmingham Reference Library*)

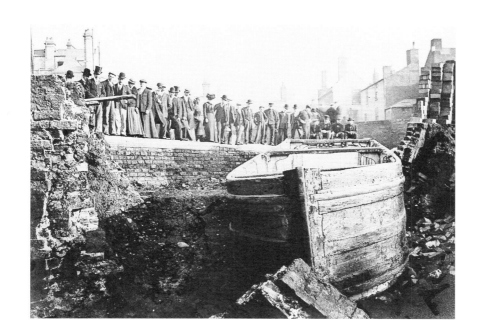

Above: Perry Barr Locks 9 & 10, Perry Barr Wharf. James Walker, engineer, managed to group eleven of the thirteen locks in a single flight. Perry Barr Wharf was placed near the bottom of the flight next to a turnpike road. There were cottages and workshops located at the wharf (right), but these were demolished and the land and basin subsequently redeveloped. Opposite this basin was the site of the Stonehouse Works (left), which was an engineering establishment. Later, Lucas converted the premises for a factory. (*Author's collection*)

Opposite top: Perry Barr Top Lock, Tame Valley Canal, 1990. This view from the Walsall Road looks down the locks towards Gravelly Hill. This canal, which was completed in 1844, created a new link to the Black Country which avoided the centre of Birmingham. The thirteen locks were arranged together in a set of two and a set of eleven, at the request of the engineering team that had James Walker at its head. The earlier parliamentary plan which distributed the locks along a curving and winding course was altered by Walker who saw it as a backwards step following the achievements of Thomas Telford on the making of the New Main Line. The impressive lock cottage is a symbol of an age when canal transport was at its peak. (*Author's collection*)

Opposite bottom: The Brookvale Destructor. During the early 1920s the Birmingham Salvage Department commenced a programme of improved rubbish collection. Part of the scheme involved the construction of destructor plants, where the rubbish was burnt and the residue taken by boat to a nearby ash tip. The first was Brookvale which was completed in 1924. Four more plants were later commissioned and all had canal-side locations: Tyseley (1926); Lifford (1930); Rotton Park (1932); and Montague Street (1935). Mr A. Pagett had a contract in 1928 to remove salvage dust by boat from the Brookvale Destructor, which was taken to his tip on the Tame Valley Canal at Perry Barr. (*Birmingham Reference Library*)

Lock 12, Deykins Avenue, Tame Valley Canal. A coal boat approaches the lock bringing a load of coal to the General Electric Company (GEC) Works at Witton. The boat horse is passing the lock cottage on the right. (*George Dale*)

The canal cottage, Lock 12, 1997. The view of the cottage as seen from Deykin Avenue bridge shows a well-kept garden associated with the cottage. Behind the cottage was the GEC Rectifier Works building that was converted to make plastic components. Linpac took over these premises to make components for the local automotive industry, but with the closure of the Rover Works, Longbridge, Linpac moved out of these premises and they were demolished. (*Author's collection*)

Above: The second lock, Farmer's Bridge, *c.* 1913. The flight of locks first descended to the Dudley Turnpike, which crossed the canal at Saturday Bridge. The towpath was lined by a number of factories and workshops. Here, in an evidently posed shot, a working boat is seen in the lock with both paddles raised. A derelict and broken old coal boat is aground in the side pound awaiting its fate. On the right are a number of buildings (including the Scotland Works), which lined the towpath of the Newhall Branch, and on the extreme right a boat is just visible tied up alongside one of the Crescent Wharf warehouses. (*Birmingham Reference Library*)

Opposite: GEC Bunker and Boiler Plant, Witton, 1993. These winter scenes show the GEC Works at Witton beside the Tame Valley Canal. Between 1,000 and 2,000 tons of coal and slack were brought each month by boat to these works. The GEC did not possess any narrowboats, but relied on factors and carriers to provide the fuel. It provided useful business for the local coal carriers, such as T. & S. Element and Leonard Leigh. A tall steel telpher can be seen beside the buildings; this was used to unload slack from boats moored below and transfer it to the stacking yard beside the boiler house. The massive bunker towered to a height of 75ft above the waterway. The plans for 1930 show that the architects and suppliers for this structure were Babcock & Wilcox. The telpher and works were demolished in the 1990s, but the boiler chimney stack was retained. (*Author's collection*)

Above: Fourth lock, Farmer's Bridge. Horses were commonly used to work day boats on the BCN up to the end of commercial carrying. On this occasion, a rubbish boat is being worked up the locks by Jeff Bennett. In this view the rubbish boat is coming out of the lock above Saturday Bridge. The horse plods on, following a regular routine without any assistance from the boatman. (*Courtesy of Jeff Bennett*)

Opposite: Farmer's Bridge Locks, 1989. The towpath from Saturday Bridge to Snow Hill was the first on this stretch to be improved and repaired. On the left is a tall factory with a pair of wood-cased hoists. The building was twice ravaged by serious fires and has now been pulled down. On the right is the surviving metal bracket which held a gas lamp to illuminate the towpath for night working. These locks were once extremely busy with both long- and short-distance traffic, which passed between upper and lower Birmingham. The BCN adopted twenty-four-hour working on the Farmer's Bridge Locks to reduce the frequent delays which occurred there. (*Author's collection*)

Above: Elkington's Works, Farmer's Bridge Locks, 1961. The tar boat *Severn*, owned by Thomas Clayton & Co., is seen passing up the locks. Elkington's had moved out of Birmingham by this date and were refining copper at Goscote. Their premises had been bought from the National Receiver by Birmingham Corporation, who established the Museum of Science and Industry on the site. (*National Waterways Museum, Ellesmere Port, Arthur Watts Collection*)

Opposite top: Newhall Street Bridge, *c.* 1913. In the days before British Telecom erected their offices and the Telecom Tower in Newhall Street, the bridge and side pound view was unobstructed. The ornate Elkington Company offices can be seen above the bridge parapets and the waterway is busy with boats. A Fellows, Morton & Clayton boat is descending, while a low cabin boat is passing into the lock under Newhall Street. There is a half-empty coal boat along the towpath. This boat was probably here to supply coal to the nearby Water Street Power Station. (*Birmingham Reference Library*)

Opposite bottom: The hotel boat *Ellesmere*, Farmer's Bridge Locks. Hotel boats are now regular sights on the rivers and canals, where they provide holidays along parts of the navigable waterways. The boats, adapted to the narrow canals, are built along traditional lines and some are ex-working boats. Usually they travel together in pairs, with a powered motorboat and an unpowered butty. On long flights of locks, such as Farmer's Bridge, the butty has to be worked through by hand using a technique called bow hauling. On this occasion the motorboat had gone ahead. One of the female crew on the *Ellesmere* is seen at the end of the rope heading under the Snow Hill station railway arch, while her two companions help to get the boat out of the lock. (*Author's collection*)

Above: Farmer's Bridge Locks, Elkington Works & Whitmore's Arm. The Elkington Electroplate factory came about through the adoption of the process of electroplating by Messrs Elkington & Mason. Elkington had taken over a former rolling mill in Newhall Street and during the 1850s considerably enlarged these premises that extended along both sides of the canal and a branch waterway known as Whitmore's Arm. The iron bridge on the left spans the entrance channel to the arm. This branch began as a simple basin, built for the landowner Lady Caroline Colmore, in order to serve the rolling mill. William James was responsible for the extension of this short basin through to Newhall Hill, where he intended to build a canal port and warehouses. William Whitmore owned the foundry at the terminus of the Newhall Branch. He was engineer to James on the Lower Stratford, 1813–16, and it seems Whitmore was also responsible for the arm that bears his name, although contemporary maps sometimes refer to the extension as the James Level. (*RCHS Hugh Compton Collection, ref. 64233*)

Opposite: Cobbles and towpath, Farmer's Bridge Flight. The hooves of countless horses and the boots of generations of boatmen have worn down the cobbles on the towpath and left an indelible record of their passing. (*Author's collection*)

Above: Snow Hill Wharf, *c.* 1913. Coal boats line the towpath opposite the BCN public wharf at Snow Hill. In this misty, smoky scene the boats near the towpath are loaded with coal destined for Summer Lane Power Station, opened in 1906. St Chad's Roman Catholic Cathedral is the dominant feature on the skyline. (*Birmingham Reference Library*)

Opposite top: Farmer's Bridge Locks. A tar boat is taken up Farmer's Bridge from Newhall Street; the boat horse is led forward to propel the boat out the lock. (*RCHS Hugh Compton Collection, ref. 64224*)

Opposite bottom: Bottom lock, Farmer's Bridge, *c.* 1905. This is a scene that has changed little over the last 100 years. Tall buildings still line the towpath on both sides. This part of the canal was industrialised at an early date. On the left was the site of an early steam rolling and flour mill, once owned by James Pickard; while on the right was George Jones's Phoenix Foundry. (*Author's collection*)

Princip Street Waterfront, 1990. The afternoon sun catches a pane of glass and highlights every ledge and brick. Clearly these premises have seen better days, but they are a reminder of the times when every room was a workshop and a host of small trades were carried out within the same building. Princip Street was located in the centre of Birmingham's gunmaking quarter and behind some of these very windows, gunmakers once carried out their art within cramped surroundings. (*Author's collection*)

Brass Foundry, Princip Street. This 1843 advert for John Scott's Brass Foundry shows a working boat on the canal. (*Author's collection*)

Aston Top Lock: a view looking down the flight. It is a scene that has changed almost completely now. The toll house and lock house on the right, and all the buildings on both sides of the canal, have gone. (*National Waterways Museum, Ellesmere Port, Arthur Watts Collection*)

Above: Aston Junction, 1961. The roving bridge carries the towpath over the Birmingham & Fazeley Canal towards and on to the Digbeth Branch. Behind the bridge is the top lock of the Aston Flight, the BCN lock house and cottage. On the right is a side bridge which spanned the entrance to an iron-sided basin. (*National Waterways Museum, Ellesmere Port, Arthur Watts Collection*)

Opposite: Aston Locks, 1983. This evening scene shows the locks before the towpath improvements of the mid-1990s. Buildings and factories still line both sides of the canal, and in the distance is the half-demolished retort house which belonged to Windsor Street Gasworks. (*Author's collection*)

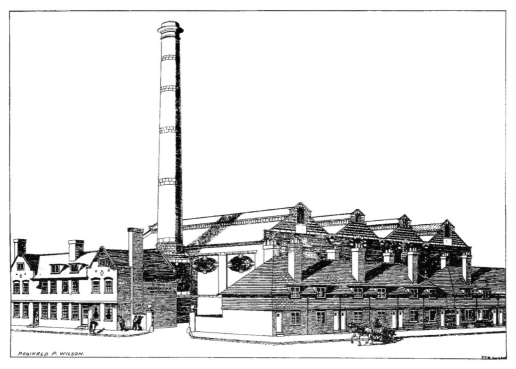

Chester Road Power Station, Aston. This is Reginald Wilson's 1900 drawing for the proposed power station at Aston. The station was completed as per the drawing in about 1902. It supplied power for electric lighting and street tramways within Aston Manor. Coal was delivered by boat alongside a wharf on the Birmingham & Fazeley Canal and taken by overhead telpher into the power station. (*Birmingham Reference Library*)

Cheston Road Wharf. The former Birmingham Corporation Stone Depot and buildings can be seen on the left behind the lock chamber. On the right is the now brick-sealed entrance to the BCN public wharf, Cheston Road. On the extreme right are another basin and the now-demolished Smith, Stone & Knight paper mills. (*Author's collection*)

Salford Junction, *c.* 1958. Today this scene has completely changed as the Gravelly Hill motorway interchange now straddles the site. The line of the Birmingham & Fazeley Canal extends from under the concrete turnover bridge across the left of the picture. The second bridge spans the Birmingham & Warwick Junction Canal, while towards the camera is the line of the Tame Valley Canal. In between the two bridges is Salford Junction toll office. The cooling towers of the new Nechells B Power Station fill the skyline. (*National Waterways Museum, Ellesmere Port, Arthur Watts Collection*)

Holly Lane Bridge, Erdington, 1931. This distinctive concrete bridge replaced a brick bridge in 1931. Note the tramway poles to the left and right of the bridge. There was a pair of tramway tracks along Holly Lane which led down to the Dunlop Works. Trams continued to use this route until 1953. (*Birmingham Reference Library*)

Ash transport on the Birmingham & Fazeley Canal, *c.* 1922. From 1900 onwards Birmingham Corporation had an increasing ash disposal problem. Ash generated by the Corporation's gas and electricity works was taken by boats to be tipped. In 1918 a new ash disposal scheme was commenced at Minworth Sewage Works. Here, a tug is towing a line of container boats along the Fazeley Canal to Minworth. (*Birmingham Reference Library*)

Minworth Wharf, *c.* 1922. Narrowboats containing ash containers were unloaded by an overhead crane, which transferred the ash boxes to bogies which ran on a 2ft gauge railway owned by the Upper Tame & Rea District Drainage Board. A pair of steam locomotives was kept at Minworth to deliver ash to the sewage works' filter beds. (*Birmingham Reference Library*)

Dunton Canal Cottages and Lock, May 1998. Here are two views of the top lock at Curdworth Flight. The group of cottages (above) were demolished in 1999 to make way for the new M6 Toll (Birmingham Northern Relief Road), which crossed the canal there. The lock (as seen below) was moved further north and the canal bed dug down to the lower level. (*Author's collection*)

Above: Thomas Clayton boat at Ashted Tunnel, 1961. Thomas Clayton operated a fleet of specially designed tar boats that collected coal tar and other chemicals from local gasworks and carried them to tar distilleries in the Oldbury and West Bromwich areas. Here, the *Severn* is seen approaching the southern portal of Ashted Tunnel having climbed up the locks from Digbeth. The Birmingham Canal had an engine house here for many years, which pumped the water back up to the top of the locks. Above the tunnel on the left was the site of the Belmont Glassworks. The wharf for the Cooperative Society Bakery is on the right. (*National Waterways Museum, Ellesmere Port, Arthur Watts Collection*)

Opposite top: Ashted Locks. The view from Belmont Row up the locks to Ashted Tunnel was one once related to industry. A central feature on the skyline is the Cooperative Society Bakery. Another structure of interest is the single- and double-storey building on the left, which was built as a Second World War decontamination centre. (*RCHS Weaver Collection, ref. 45291*)

Opposite bottom: Proof house, Digbeth Branch, 1997. The proof house was erected in 1813 to test guns manufactured by the Birmingham gunmaking community. This building still stands and continues as a gun proof house. The boats in the foreground were engaged in environmental dredging work. (*Author's collection*)

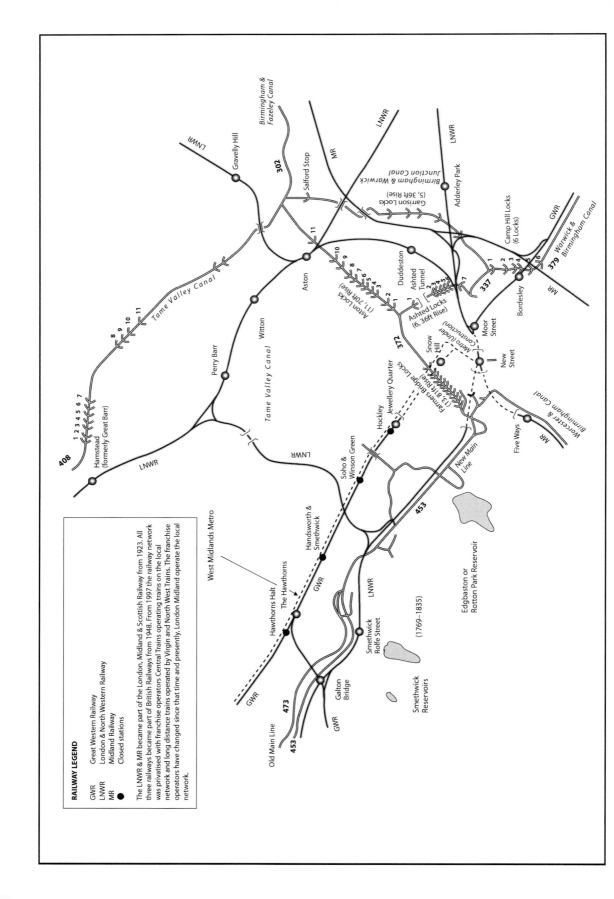

RAILWAY LEGEND

GWR   Great Western Railway
LNWR   London & North Western Railway
MR   Midland Railway
●   Closed stations

The LNWR & MR became part of the London, Midland & Scottish Railway from 1923. All three railways became part of British Railways from 1948. From 1997 the railway network was privatised with franchise operators Central Trains operating trains on the local network and long distance trains operated by Virgin and North West Trains. The franchise operators have changed since that time and presently, London Midland operate the local network.

West Midlands Metro

2

Worcester & Birmingham Canal

The Worcester & Birmingham Canal was proposed during the time of Britain's greatest canal expansion. It was a bold plan to unite Birmingham and the River Severn at Worcester with a canal wide enough to take barges. John Snape was commissioned to survey the route in 1789. The promoters of the scheme had a difficult task ahead of them. Local canal companies, such as the Staffordshire & Worcestershire, feared the proposed canal from Worcester to Birmingham would take trade from their canal. In fact, the first bill before Parliament in 1790 was successfully opposed by the companies with vested interests to keep the status quo. There were, however, many supporters keen to see the canal built, and in 1791 the Worcester & Birmingham Canal Act was passed, enabling construction to commence.

Having the authority to build was a long way from getting the work completed. The Worcester & Birmingham Canal proprietors endured many problems before completion in December 1815. Work was conducted in stages starting at the Birmingham end and progressing towards Selly Oak and then Kings Norton. Construction began in 1792 after the canal was re-surveyed. Snape found that a saving of 2 miles could be achieved from his previous plan. The canal company began staking out the ground, purchasing barrows, carts and horses and erecting brick kilns. Bricks, at this time, were handmade from local clays, which were fired in kilns near the canal. The task of cutting the canal was given to Mr Morecroft, whose first contract was to make the canal navigable for flats (basic vessels) between the turnpike road at Five Ways to the north side of the Bournbrook Valley. This was followed by other contracts that extended through Kings Norton to Hopwood.

Canal construction proceeded by the length, which was measured up before the digging started. When sections were completed, water was let in and these parts were used by flats to move spoil, bricks and lime. Canal cutting was purely physical. Labourers, called navvies, or navigators, dug out the canal by pick and shovel. The Worcester & Birmingham Canal did not follow the land contours, as the Old Birmingham Canal had done, but was made across valleys and through hillsides and kept to the same level. There was much more work involved to build a canal of this nature. Embankments had to be made and cuttings excavated, all to the dimensions of a barge canal. Soon Morecroft had a large workforce on the job. The authority to build barracks, at Edgbaston Hall Deep Cutting, Bournbrook Valley and Gallows Brook Valley, was approved by the canal company in December 1792. Another barracks near John Wheeley's house was sanctioned the following month. As each barracks was designed for 100 men, some 400 men must have been employed on the works at the start of 1793. The construction of Edgbaston Tunnel, and later West Hill Tunnel, involved the sinking of shafts and digging out the tunnel along the intended line until all sections were joined up. Horse gins were used by the sinkers to bring spoils to the surface from the excavations and to take bricks down below to the bricklayers employed to make the tunnel sides.

The canal was officially opened to Selly Oak on 30 October 1795 and by May 1796 had reached Lifford. Meanwhile, West Hill Tunnel was nearing completion. Work on this tunnel had started in 1793, but was not finished until 1797. Five gins and a portable steam engine were used on this contract. A barracks capable of holding fifty men was erected on nearby wasteland in 1795, and six brick kilns were needed to make the bricks for the tunnel. By the end of March 1797 the Worcester & Birmingham Canal was opened to Hopwood. The carriage of coal was considered an important cargo and carrying companies were set up to take coal to Hockley (Stratford upon Avon Canal) and Hopwood. A packet boat operated for a short time between Hopwood and Worcester Wharf, Birmingham. This boat, called *Speedwell*, which carried both passengers and parcels, began operating on 9 August 1798. It ran three days a week, on Mondays, Thursdays and Fridays, leaving Hopwood at 7 a.m. and returning from Birmingham at 4 p.m. Calls were made at Kings Norton and Selly Oak. The advertised journey time was two and a half hours. Only one hour was allowed for the journey between Kings Norton and Hopwood, which included the passage through West Hill Tunnel.

Financing the work was a constant problem and further cutting proceeded slowly towards Tardebigge. The waterway from Birmingham had maintained a constant height of 453ft, which is the same as at Gas Street and Telford's deep cutting through Smethwick. However, the Worcester & Birmingham Canal was not permitted to join the Birmingham Canal at Gas Street. A physical bar just over 7ft wide meant that all goods had to be transhipped across the bar.

The Worcester & Birmingham Canal Company had a large wharf area in Birmingham which they gradually developed as trade increased. The L-shaped piece of land which became known as Worcester Wharf extended on both sides of the canal from the Bar as far as Granville Street, and was bounded by Bridge Street, Gas Street and Commercial Road. Their new offices were built near Commercial Road facing Worcester Wharf. As the land dipped towards Bridge Street, the wharf land and new canal had to be built up to the same level as Gas Street Basin.

A barge canal had been maintained throughout which could accept 14ft-wide craft capable of carrying 60 to 80 tons at a time. When the waterway opened to Kings Norton, the carrier John Wall used at least one wide boat for trading purposes. Tardebigge was reached at the end of March 1807. Beyond Tardebigge the land drops steadily towards the River Severn. The original hope of a wide canal to the river was to prove too costly. Further progress was halted until the means of going forward was decided. Experiments with a boat lift proved unsuccessful and eventually work went ahead with the construction of fifty-eight locks to the Severn at Diglis. All but the last two locks were made to narrowboat dimensions. Through traffic thus became confined to narrowboats, which commenced trading along the whole canal from Diglis to Birmingham in December 1815. The year 1815 was also marked by the passing of the Act that permitted a lock at Worcester Bar, which enabled through traffic between the Worcester & Birmingham and the Birmingham Canal Navigations.

The construction and promotion of the Worcester & Birmingham Canal had also encouraged other canal links. The Stratford upon Avon Canal joined at Lifford, while at Selly Oak there was the junction with the Dudley Canal. Once completed, the line of the Worcester & Birmingham Canal changed little compared with the vast improvements that were carried out along the BCN. The most significant changes were with the wharves and canal-side industry. In Birmingham, Worcester Wharf was developed and enlarged on the Bridge Street side. Here were timber wharves and a number of carriers' warehouses. The other important wharves along this waterway were located at Tardebigge, Stoke Prior, Hanbury, Lowesmere (Lowesmoor) and Diglis.

Industry along the Worcester & Birmingham Canal was never as concentrated as on other Birmingham canals. There were sites, however, which contributed to trade on the canal. They included Sturge's Chemical Works in Bath Row, Elliott's Copper Works at Selly Oak, Cadbury's chocolate factory at Bournville, Baldwin's paper factory at Lifford and the Kings Norton Metal Works.

Between 1864 and 1865 the company offices were moved to Gas Street. Here they occupied a new building constructed over the entrance to Netherton Basin. Netherton Basin had been originally built for the proprietors of the Dudley Canal Company, who had leased the land chiefly as a coal wharf for the trade from Netherton along the Dudley Canal into Birmingham, but also accommodated canal carriers who traded along the Dudley, Stratford and Worcester & Birmingham Canals. It was, in fact, a detached piece of the Dudley Canal in the heart of Birmingham. Further changes took place when the Worcester & Birmingham Canal amalgamated with the Sharpness Canal Company in 1874, becoming the Sharpness New Docks & Gloucester & Birmingham Navigations Company. It remained a busy trading route, particularly for the Severn & Canal Carrying Company (SCCC), whose boats worked the length of the Severn through Worcester to the Bridge Street warehouses.

Bridge Street Depot was still used by British Waterways for most of the 1950s, but was demolished in the 1970s. The modern wharf hotel and restaurant now occupies the site. Further residential developments also occurred, followed by the redevelopment of a 1970s Royal Mail sorting office as the Mailbox. Retail units and offices filled the vacated site and the BBC moved their radio and television studios from Pebble Mill to here. The former Corporation's stone and salvage depot at Holliday Street was converted into mixed leisure, residential and office use, and the site now includes the Registry Office, which had been relocated from Broad Street. Sadly, the developers for this project chose to demolish all the buildings save for the facade facing the canal. Arguably, a more serious loss of heritage was the demolition of the old Granville Street Wharf, the Washington Foundry buildings and the facade of the Adamant Plaster Works. While British Waterways decided to remove Granville Street Wharf to build a fish restaurant, this change proved to be temporary when planning permission was given for the development of the 'Cube'. Although fated to be delayed by various issues, the building and fitting out of the Cube went ahead and now the completed structure dominates the neighbourhood, casting a long and dark shadow at times over the waterway and people's homes alike. Though praised by some as an architectural marvel, there are opposing voices of dissent. It is a structure that is best described as being built in the wrong place and perhaps the wrong city. Gaudy and garish, the Cube may be an award winner, but it could also be described as an eyesore.

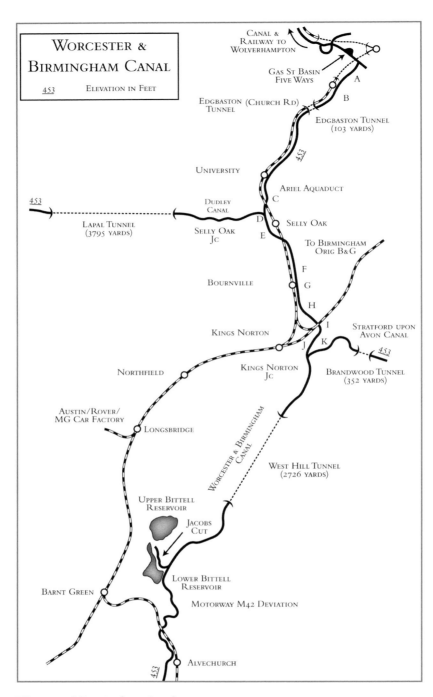

WORCESTER & BIRMINGHAM CANAL

453 — ELEVATION IN FEET

CANAL & RAILWAY TO WOLVERHAMPTON

GAS ST BASIN FIVE WAYS

A

B

EDGBASTON (CHURCH RD) TUNNEL

EDGBASTON TUNNEL (103 YARDS)

453

UNIVERSITY

ARIEL AQUADUCT

C

453

DUDLEY CANAL

D

SELLY OAK

LAPAL TUNNEL (3795 YARDS)

SELLY OAK JC

E

TO BIRMINGHAM ORIG B&G

F

BOURNVILLE

G

H

I

STRATFORD UPON AVON CANAL

KINGS NORTON

K

J

453

NORTHFIELD

KINGS NORTON JC

BRANDWOOD TUNNEL (352 YARDS)

AUSTIN/ROVER/ MG CAR FACTORY

LONGSBRIDGE

WORCESTER & BIRMINGHAM CANAL

WEST HILL TUNNEL (2726 YARDS)

UPPER BITTELL RESERVOIR

JACOBS CUT

LOWER BITTELL RESERVOIR

BARNT GREEN

MOTORWAY M42 DEVIATION

453

ALVECHURCH

Worcester & Birmingham Canal.

A   Davenports Brewery
B   Sturges Chemical Works
C   Components/Ariel Cycle Works
D   Birmingham Battery Works
E   Elliot's Copper Works
F   Cadbury's Waterside Wharf

G   Cadbury's Mary Vale Road Wharf
H   GKN Screw Works
I   Lifford Salvage Depot
J   Lifford Chemical Works/Kings
    Norton Metal Works
K   Baldwin's Paper Mill

Worcester Bar, 1913. For twenty years the Worcester Bar provided a physical barrier between the BCN and the Worcester & Birmingham Canal. All goods had to be transhipped across the barrier or through the wharves on either side. In 1815 a stop lock was constructed which allowed boats to pass through. The Worcester & Birmingham Canal was obliged to raise its level 6in so that there was less chance of water being lost from the Birmingham Canal. Contemporary plans show that there were also two gates at either end of the lock chamber, in case the levels changed. A narrowboat is seen in the lock with the paddle gear raised. There are also a number of narrowboats moored side by side with their bows against the bar. Behind the boats is a range of canal-side buildings, some of which still survive. (*Birmingham Reference Library*)

Worcester Bar, 1990. During the 1990s many alterations were made to the canal side around Worcester Bar and Gas Street Basin, but it is still a place where traditional narrowboats can be seen. Here, motor and butty boats are moored alongside each other in a fashion little changed since the early days of canal carrying. In the background, work is progressing on the ICC and there is scaffolding around one of the canal-side buildings. This latter building was reconstructed as the Glassworks public house, which takes its name from a nearby flint glassworks. (*Author's collection*)

Worcester Bar and Bar Lock, 1992. The Bar Lock had two toll offices side by side, one for the Worcester & Birmingham, the other for the BCN. The Worcester & Birmingham Canal office was constructed in 1893 to replace an earlier office which had fallen into disrepair. When this picture was taken, the toll office had become an antiques shop, which later closed and after a period of disuse became a British Waterways Information Office, then offices. Next to the Worcester & Birmingham Canal toll office was the two-storey Birmingham Canal toll office of 1815. This building is now converted into a coffee shop. After the canal system came under the control of British Waterways, the Worcester & Birmingham Canal was made the same level as the Birmingham Canal and the (four) lock gates were left permanently open. People wishing to cross the lock to the Worcester Bar, who would previously have used the lock gates, had to make do with a wooden plank. In 1988 a new cast-iron bridge was constructed to span the Bar Lock. (*Author's collection*)

No. 4 Worcester Wharf, Bridge Street, *c.* 1880. Canal-side wharf buildings could either be of timber or brick construction. Those buildings on No. 4 were originally made chiefly of timber, as this sketch shows. They had been used by Pickford & Co. who leased both wharf space and warehouses here. When Pickford's transferred their main carrying trade to the railways, Joshua Fellows started to use the premises. Joshua Fellows was one of the founding members of Fellows, Morton & Clayton, but he also carried on the trade to Worcester and the River Severn as a separate business. Joshua was assisted in this venture by his brother James. Later, the Fellows brothers were to join with Danks, Venn & Co. to set up the Severn & Canal Carrying Company. In the foreground is the cabin of a butty belonging to John Boys of Walsall. (*Birmingham Reference Library*)

Worcester Wharf, *c.* 1930. The Severn & Canal Carrying Company Motorboat No. 1 is seen reversing into position beside Worcester Wharf. No. 1, which was built by the Anderton Company, Middleport, entered service with the SCCC in 1927. (*Railway Canal & Historical Society*)

Worcester Wharf, Bridge Street, 1930s. The SCCC Bridge Street Wharf comprised three wharves, Nos 3–5, which had originally been leased to different carriers. The premises were amalgamated and a long brick warehouse replaced the original buildings along the canal side. A wooden canopy extended along the front of the warehouse to provide shelter for the boats while they loaded or unloaded. These two views show motors and butties tied up alongside the wharf. (*Railway Canal & Historical Society*)

Above: Holliday Street Aqueduct, 1994. The Worcester & Birmingham Canal crosses Holliday Street by an elegant brick and iron aqueduct, supported by a row of iron piers. This aqueduct replaced the original brick structure in 1885 as part of the Worcester Wharf reconstruction (1882–85). There had been a narrow passageway called the Gullet which passed under the canal and through Worcester Wharf to Wharf Street. There were many rundown houses, hovels and tenements in the Gullet and surrounding streets. Here, too, were alehouses where the boatmen would spend their wages and sometimes seek out local prostitutes. The whole area was changed when the Midland Railway built a new rail link through to New Street station and constructed Central Goods station. The railway work caused part of Worcester Wharf to be reconstructed and at the same time Holliday Street was extended under the canal and through to Suffolk Street. (*Author's collection*)

Opposite top: Worcester Wharf, Bridge Street, 1930s. The wharf had a number of hoists and cranes to assist the loading and unloading of goods. Here, metal bars are being unloaded by the crane. A number of Typhoo tea boxes remain in the boat. (*Railway Canal & Historical Society*)

Opposite bottom: Worcester Wharf, Bridge Street, 1930s. Canal warehouses were busy places, with boxes and barrels stacked in every conceivable corner. (*Railway Canal & Historical Society*)

Above: Worcester Wharf, Bridge Street, 1930s. A SCCC road lorry is being loaded with Typhoo tea boxes at the rear of the wharf. (*Railway Canal & Historical Society*)

Opposite top: Granville Street Wharf, 1913. The main line of the Worcester & Birmingham Canal makes a 90-degree turn after crossing Holliday Street. It then passes under a series of road bridges on the way to Selly Oak. The first is Granville Street Bridge, where there were wharves on both sides of the canal. The wharf on the left is stacked with sanitary ware and chimney pots: this was Doulton's Granville Street Wharf. Doulton's manufactured salt-glazed pottery at Smethwick and Rowley Regis, and it was brought by boat to this wharf. On the right, a number of coal boats are moored up alongside the cobbled towpath. Here, on the right, was Birmingham Corporation's Holliday Street Stone Yard and Salvage Wharf. The buildings form part of the stable block. (*Birmingham Reference Library*)

Opposite bottom: Davenports Brewery and Cemetery Sidings. The scene from Granville Street Bridge has changed within the last few years. Davenports Brewery occupied the site on the left of the canal, which is now housing. On the right is the boundary wall between the railway and the canal. There was a railway sidings on the opposite side of the wall called Cemetery Sidings. It was known as such because there was once a Jewish burial ground near this spot. (*Author's collection*)

The Cube, Worcester Wharf, Granville Street, 2012. Granville Street Wharf, which once housed a group of heritage buildings, including the former Doulton's Pipe Wharf and Washington Foundry, has now been covered by some controversial modern structures. The dominant feature is the Cube, which has been praised by some and condemned by others. (*Author's collection*)

Edgbaston Tunnel. The Worcester & Birmingham Canal passes through a short cutting and tunnel which takes the waterway under Church Road. This tunnel, which now has a towpath, was originally made wide enough to allow wide boat or barge traffic to pass. There would have been an even slope down to the towpath when the canal first opened, but this was changed in 1876 when the West Suburban Railway was opened from Kings Norton to Granville Street station. Part of the canal land was given up to build the railway, and navigation and towpath moved a few yards to the east. Normally, the towpath would curve away from the tunnel mouth: here it can be seen to run straight. The West Suburban Railway was a single-line railway which closely followed the route of the canal. The Midland Railway Company rebuilt this line in 1882 and 1885, making it a double track and straightening certain sections in the process. The tall brick-lined railway cutting, seen on the left, was done as part of this later work. (*Author's collection*)

Above: Bristol Road Bridge, 1999. The Bristol Road crosses the Worcester & Birmingham Canal at Selly Oak. It was once a turnpike road and later a tramway route. Dominating the skyline is the former Birmingham Battery Works, which now comprises a group of industrial units. There was a coal merchant's wharf through the bridge on the right; this is now a builder's merchant's yard. (*Author's collection*)

Opposite top: Davenports Brewery buildings. This image shows the Worcester & Birmingham Canal towards Granville Street Bridge. A Birmingham & Midland Canal Carrying Company motor and butty are seen passing the brewery with a number of children on board, en route to a camping holiday. (*Author's collection*)

Opposite bottom: Viaduct and Aqueduct at Selly Oak, August 2011. When the Worcester & Birmingham Canal was constructed, one engineering challenge was the crossing of the Bourn Brook Valley. This brook, which is seen at the bottom of the photograph, joined the River Rea. The contractors for the barge canal, Morecroft & Co., made a tall and wide embankment to cross the valley over the brook. A parallel railway embankment was later constructed for the single-track West Suburban Railway from Kings Norton to Granville Street (by contractor John Aird), and this embankment was altered and widened by Joseph Firbank's men when the Midland Railway improved the railway and extended it into Birmingham (New Street). During 2010 the planning of a new road through to the new Queen Elizabeth Hospital led to the construction of a concrete aqueduct and concrete viaduct. In order for navigation to be maintained on the canal, a temporary canal diversion was made, cutting through the towing path, and a temporary lift bridge was installed for contractors' vehicles to cross the canal channel. Once the concrete structures were in place, the spoil and earth was dug out for the road. The railway viaduct (foreground) is numbered as Bridge 18A. The canal aqueduct (behind) was named Ariel to commemorate the former bicycle and motorcycle factory that once occupied the site through which the road passes. (*Author's collection*)

Above: Cadbury No. 10, Waterside Factory. One of Cadbury Brothers' own locomotives shunts wagons beside the canal, 1955. (*Roger Carpenter Collection*)

Below: Pershore Road, Breedon Cross, 1993. The towpath was diverted on to the opposite bank to allow for the construction of Lifford Railway Interchange Wharf. There is now a modern turnover bridge which takes the towpath across from the railway to the far side. (*Author's collection*)

Cadbury's Ltd, Waterside Wharf. The firm of Cadbury Brothers made chocolate in a canal-side factory beside the Old Wharf, Bridge Street, Birmingham. They relocated to larger premises in Bournville in 1879. A canal wharf was established beside the Worcester & Birmingham Canal near Vale Road Bridge. Cadbury's built up an important trade where milk converted into crumb was brought by boat to the Bournville works. The Waterside Wharf, opened in 1925, replaced the earlier premises off Vale Road. It was served by an internal railways system, which connected the wharf to the main works. In this view several SCCC boats can be seen moored alongside the Waterside Wharf. The wharf premises survived the cessation of canal traffic and remained until the early 1980s. They have since been pulled down and houses have been built on the site. (*Railway Canal & Historical Society*)

Lifford Railway Interchange Wharf. A SCCC Motorboat MV4 can be seen towing two butties past Lifford Railway Depot. Here, goods were transferred between railway trucks and boats owned by the Midland (later LMS) Railway Company. Interchange traffic ceased here in 1927. This picture dates from the late 1920s or early 1930s, after Lifford Wharf had closed. Motor No. 4 was one of two SCCC boats to bear this fleet number. The first had been purchased from Cadbury Brothers in 1928 and had previously been known as Bournville No. 2. The second was a butty boat conversion in 1933. Canal carrying on the Worcester & Birmingham Canal had begun to decline by 1930. The SCCC decided to concentrate their business on the River Severn trade, using larger vessels which transferred their goods to road vehicles at Stourport and Worcester. In 1942 the SCCC changed their name to the Severn Carrying Company Ltd. A much-reduced narrowboat fleet was retained until the takeover by the Docks & Inland Waterways Executive in 1948. (*Railway & Canal Historical Society*)

Above: Kings Norton Paper Mills, Lifford. A number of coal boats can be seen moored beside the mill's wharf. These paper mills were established by James Baldwin & Sons and later operated by Kings Norton Paper Mills Ltd. James Baldwin first made paper at the Sherborne Mill in Birmingham, but later transferred his operation to the Lifford site where the new mills were also called the Sherborne Mills. A mixture of wood fibre and rags were boiled together to produce the pulp which made the paper. A considerable amount of waste material, including cloth, rags and waste paper, were recycled in this way. James Baldwin produced a range of paper products, including the traditional blue writing paper and brown paper for grocers' bags. Coal, chiefly slack, was an essential part of the paper-making process, fuelling the boilers for the mills. It was brought to the works by boat from mines such as those at Cannock Chase or Sandwell Park. Kings Norton Paper Mills Ltd usually paid all the tolls for traffic. (*Colin Scrivener, courtesy of the National Waterways Museum, Ellesmere Port*)

Opposite top: Lifford Salvage Works, 1930. This was a canal-side feature on the towpath side of the Worcester & Birmingham Canal, south of Lifford Railway Wharf. It was first built in 1906 by Kings Norton Urban District Council, but was subsequently enlarged by Birmingham Corporation in 1930. (*Author's collection*)

Opposite bottom: Kings Norton Junction. The Worcester & Birmingham Canal toll house, Kings Norton Junction, faced the Stratford Canal. It remains an imposing canal-side feature. The spire of Kings Norton parish church is visible in the distance. (*Author's collection*)

A group of SCCC butty narrowboats are seen passing along the Worcester & Birmingham Canal near West Hill Tunnel, Kings Norton, each boat being hauled by its own horse. In later years the SCCC would use motorboats to tow the butty boats. (*National Waterways Museum, Ellesmere Port*)

West Hill Tunnel, North Portal. Kings Norton has two canal tunnels: one at Brandwood (Stratford upon Avon Canal) and one at West Hill (Worcester & Birmingham Canal). Both tunnels were designed by the same engineer, Josiah Clowes, although there are differences in the portal brickwork. This view has been identified as the north portal of the West Hill Tunnel. The south portal has a rather basic entrance. (*Birmingham Reference Library*)

3

Stratford Upon Avon Canal

The Stratford upon Avon Canal joins the Worcester & Birmingham Canal at Lifford and passes through Shirley, Earlswood, Hockley Heath, Wootton Wawen and Wilmcote before reaching the River Avon at Stratford upon Avon. This canal was completed in stages and as finances permitted. Cutting began in 1793 at the Lifford end, and by May 1796 the new waterway had been opened to Hockley Heath. This first piece of canal was built wide enough to accommodate barges. Construction restarted in 1799 and the second section was opened to Kingswood, near Lapworth, in May 1802. The descent to Kingswood involved the construction of locks which for economic reasons were made narrow; thus, any plans for barge operation beyond Hockley Heath were prevented. A link was made with the Warwick & Birmingham Canal at Kingswood and through traffic to Birmingham via the Stratford and Worcester & Birmingham Canals was made possible for the first time.

Once the Kingswood link had been finished, certain canal carriers used this canal to access private wharves in Birmingham adjoining the main Worcester Wharf. The route was more direct than that via Camp Hill, Digbeth and the Birmingham & Fazeley Canal.

Kingswood remained the terminus of the Stratford Canal for ten years. In 1812 work started on completing the third (and last) part, through to the Avon, which was reached in June 1816.

Industrial development was less concentrated than on other navigations. Near Kings Heath, a basin was made to serve a coal wharf and limekilns. Later, at Solihull Lodge, an aluminium refinery was built where aluminium was extracted chemically. The cost of moving acid by canal soon led to the relocation of these works to Oldbury, where the acids were made and transport costs were less. The last factory to move to the Stratford Canal was Sturge's, who constructed a works for producing fine quality calcium carbonate in Lifford Lane.

The Stratford never saw as many boats as other local canals, but trade was always busiest on the northern part between Kings Norton and Kingswood. Traffic declined after the Stratford was purchased by the Oxford, Worcester & Wolverhampton Railway in 1856. It remained in railway ownership until nationalisation, being owned and maintained by the Great Western Railway for much of that time.

Some traders continued to use the northern Stratford, but even this had all but ceased by 1945. The period of ensuing dereliction might have sealed its fate, but campaigners, such as Tom Rolt and fellow members of the Inland Waterways Association, generated public interest in this waterway. In 1956 the Stratford upon Avon Canal Society was formed. Their members and members of the Coventry Canal Society made sterling efforts to ensure restoration. Warwickshire County Council in the meantime wanted the southern section to be abandoned, but the National Trust stepped in during 1960 and purchased the southern section from Kingswood to Stratford and commenced restoration work. This work was carried out between 1961 and 1964, with David Hutchins in charge as the director of operations. Restoration was carried out on not only the southern part but also the northern part, which remained in British Waterways' ownership. Restoration work on the Upper Avon Navigation has now made the Stratford Canal a popular route for boaters. Narrowboats regularly make the trip down the full length of the Stratford (the lower Stratford Canal was handed back to British Waterways in 1988) and on to the Avon. They frequently follow the Avon Ring to Tewkesbury, to travel along the Severn and Worcester & Birmingham Canal, a route that includes the punishing ascent or descent of the locks at Tardebigge.

Lifford Stop Lock and Toll House, early 1900s. The Stop Lock at Kings Norton provided the physical barrier to navigation between the Stratford upon Avon Canal and the Worcester & Birmingham Canal. Here, boats passing from the Worcester & Birmingham Canal on to the Stratford Canal were expected to pay the tolls to the Stratford Canal Company. A boat can be seen passing through the lock while a number of people look down from Lifford Lane Bridge, perhaps marking some special event. The toll house and canal-side cottage (of 1797), visible on the towpath side, have now been demolished. (*National Waterways Museum, Ellesmere Port*)

The Guillotine Stop Gates, Lifford. It seems that when the canal first opened in 1796, there was a different arrangement of the stop gates and lock at Lifford. Company records suggest that the gates were of the conventional type and the lock chamber was wide enough to pass a barge. A lock of this width required pairs of mitre gates. In fact, the company minutes record for 26 May 1798 that the mitres of the stop lock gates should be leathered as soon as possible to prevent loss of water. By April 1814 the Lifford stop gates were in urgent need of repair. It was decided to replace them with new gates of an improved design proposed by Mr Whitmore. At the same time the lock was to be reduced in width to the dimension of a boat, i.e. narrowboat. The number of gates was also to be reduced to two, implying that there had been four sets on the original stop as prescribed by the original Act of Parliament. The present Lifford guillotine gates, therefore, may well date from 1814, when cast ironwork could have been produced by Whitmore's iron foundry in Birmingham. The gate shown here is in the lower position, preventing passage into the lock. Since nationalisation both gates have been left permanently raised. (*Birmingham Reference Library*)

Above: Lifford Lane and Lifford Stop Lock, 1960. The canal cottage was still standing in this view and all lock gearing for the guillotine gates in place. (*RCHS Weaver Collection, ref. 65524*)

Opposite: Lifford Stop. The old canal bridge over the Stop in Lifford Lane Bridge was taken down and replaced by a modern bridge. During reconstruction work pedestrians were provided with a temporary scaffold footbridge to cross the canal. Both gates can be seen in this photograph; normally one would be obscured by the bridge. (*Author's collection*)

Above: Brandwood Tunnel, West Portal. The Stratford upon Avon Canal has one tunnel which passes through the hillside at Brandwood. The canal tunnel was 16ft wide – a breadth fit for barge traffic – and was made to the specifications of engineer Josiah Clowes. The tunnel was finished in 1796, a year after Clowes died. (*RCHS Hugh Compton Collection, photographer Philip Weaver, ref. 65527*)

Opposite: Tunnel Lane Drawbridge. The terms 'drawbridge' and 'lift bridge' are applied to bridges which are raised by a chain or a winch mechanism. The Tunnel Lane bridge crossed the Stratford Canal near Lifford Chemical Works. Here, a horse and cart is crossing the bridge, which in this photograph is in its original state. Later, in about 1945, the woodwork had deteriorated to such an extent that the bridge was left permanently down, the lift mechanism disconnected, with steel decking in place of the wood. This might have been enough to close the canal had it not been for the efforts of Tom Rolt. At the time boats had a statutory right to navigate canals which had not been formally abandoned, and the northern Stratford was still an open canal. In 1947 Rolt gave notice to the Great Western Railway, the then owners of the Stratford Canal, of his intention to pass along it from Kingswood to Kings Norton. The railway company had to comply and sent a team of engineers to jack up the bridge to permit Rolt's boat, *Cressy*, to pass. This was followed by the demands of other boaters who wished the waterway to be kept open and the drawbridge was replaced by a new swing bridge. (*Birmingham Reference Library*)

Above: Millpool Hill Bridge, Kings Heath, 1939. The Alcester Road crosses the Stratford Canal at Millpool Hill Bridge (No. 3). During 1939 the old brick bridge was taken down and replaced with a wider concrete structure. In this shot the canal has been drained and the footings for the new bridge are taking shape. On the left, behind the bridge, is the Horseshoe Inn, which still stands. Previous owners of this public house have been coal and lime merchants. Behind the inn is a basin which formerly served a coal wharf and limekilns. (*Birmingham Reference Library*)

Opposite top: The River Cole Aqueduct, July 1999. The Stratford Canal crosses the River Cole near Shirley via a brick aqueduct. There is room for both the river and the single-track Aqueduct Road to pass under the canal. (*Author's collection*)

Opposite bottom: Shirley Drawbridge, July 1999. The Stratford Canal is a popular route for boaters who either pass along the northern section or complete the whole journey through to Stratford upon Avon. Bridge 8 is a modern steel drawbridge which replaced an earlier wooden structure. It used to be worked by boat crews who raised and lowered the bridge using a windlass. The windlass turned a hydraulic mechanism, which was common for these bridges and some lock gates. This road became a popular route for motorists and British Waterways subsequently installed traffic lights and a mechanically operated system that is activated by a BW key. (*Author's collection*)

Three May Poles Wharf, Dickens Heath. The old bridge was a typical brick, hump-backed structure. Yet this bridge has a channel wide enough for a barge to pass, unlike the bridges south of Hockley Heath where the canal was only built for narrowboat traffic. (*RCHS Hugh Compton Collection, photographer Philip Weaver, ref. 65529*)

4

Dudley Canal

The Dudley Canal joined the Birmingham Canal Navigations at Tipton, the Stourbridge Canal at the Delph and the Worcester & Birmingham Canal at Selly Oak. The Dudley, like the Birmingham, provided a useful through route to other waterways. The Dudley Canal passed through the coalfield and had numerous coal and ironworks. Limestone mines also communicated directly with the Dudley Canal and the waterway was frequently busy with mineral traffic.

Only part of Dudley Canal (No. 2) extended into Greater Birmingham, which was the section from Lapal Tunnel to Selly Oak. This part was completed in May 1798 and enabled coal traffic from the Netherton collieries to reach Birmingham by way of the Worcester & Birmingham Canal. The Lapal to Selly Oak section was essentially rural, but coal and limestone wharves were soon established near the junction at Selly Oak. They were followed by a boat-building yard run by a member of the Monk family. A brick works was later established at California near Lapal Tunnel. There was a brief period of packet boat operation from Netherton to Birmingham which commenced at the end of August 1798. The industry packet boat was scheduled to complete the journey in four hours!

Lapal Tunnel (3,795yd) was the longest canal tunnel in the West Midlands. It was lined throughout by bricks and required frequent maintenance. During the early years of operation the tunnel was shut because of subsidence. There was no towpath and all boats had to be legged or poled through. Boats could take up to three hours to pass through, which limited traffic on this stretch. In 1841 the Dudley Canal Company provided a steam engine at the Halesowen end, which operated a scoop wheel. The wheel generated a current in the Selly Oak direction thereby assisting boats to pass through. The scoop also slightly raised the water level in the canal between two strategically placed stop gates (one by the engine, the other at Weoley Castle). Releasing the water at the Halesowen end was enough to reverse the current and assist the boats coming from Selly Oak.

In 1846 the Dudley Canal Company was merged with BCN, which operated the Dudley Canal as part of their system. Lapal Tunnel continued to have problems: it almost closed in 1912, but was repaired; however, a final roof fall in 1917 sealed its fate for good. Boats could navigate to both ends of Lapal Tunnel but not pass through. The canal at the Selly Oak end still saw traffic passing to the Stonehouse Brickworks and the Battery Works. Harborne Lane Wharf and Monks boatyard were virtually obliterated when Harborne

Lane was widened in 1928. Thereafter, the Selly Oak end continued to deteriorate and was finally abandoned in 1953.

While the entrance to Lapal Tunnel has been filled in and landscaped, the route from Lapal to Selly Oak Junction has survived without serious obstruction, and a section within Selly Oak Park still holds water. Spurred on by the success of other contemporary waterway projects, a restoration scheme to bring the canal back into use – the Lapal Canal Trust – was set up in 1990. They were keen to restore use to both the closed section and the tunnel. A length of canal was relined with concrete in Leasowes Park, Halesowen, but nothing has been done at the Selly Oak end. A few years ago, the Battery Works were demolished and the site was set aside for redevelopment as a Sainsbury's supermarket. Harborne Lane was also altered as part of new roadworks serving the Queen Elizabeth Hospital. A new bridge over the canal bed was provided with sufficient headroom for boats.

In the long time since its formation, the Trust has faced many obstacles, such as replacing canal crossings at busy roads, but the early and ambitious part of their scheme was a widened canal tunnel lined with concrete throughout. After studies and reports, such proposals were sidelined in favour of yet another ambitious project: the building of the canal over the summit using locks. During 2011 the intended Sainsbury's development at Selly Oak threatened to block the navigation route, where previously there had been a sympathetic proposal for a section of waterway to be included in the plans. Fresh provisions have now been made for a channel for the boaters on the now-demolished Battery Works site, where Sainsbury's intend to build their new store.

Harborne Lane Bridge, 1922. Harborne Lane in Selly Oak crossed the Dudley Canal by a narrow brick bridge. The photograph is looking along the towpath from near the Stop Lock. Through the bridge was a coal merchant's wharf and basin. (*Birmingham Reference Library*)

Above: Harborne Lane Wharf, 1929. Work had begun on altering the canal prior to bridge reconstruction and road widening. Harborne Lane crossed the canal and passed to the left of the picture. Where the men are working was the BCN Canal Wharf. On the right of the bridge the canal cottage has been demolished and the basin has been filled in. In the background are the three chimneys of the Birmingham Battery Works. (*Birmingham Reference Library*)

Right: Lapal Tunnel and California Inn. The eastern portal for the Lapal Tunnel was located at California, near Weoley Castle. This tunnel was opened to traffic in May 1798. Narrowboats passed through the tunnel until 1917 when a roof fall prevented any further navigation. The canal had little traffic to this point thereafter, although boats continued to come up from Selly Oak to serve Smart's California brick works, whose basin entrance is seen on the right. After a lengthy period of dereliction, the tunnel entrance was covered up and the whole area landscaped and levelled, completely obliterating any visible trace of the canal here. (*Birmingham Reference Library*)

Smart's Brickworks, 1941. Bricks were manufactured from various local clays which were quarried, ground and moulded before being fired in a kiln. Brick kilns were once common canal-side features. The buildings include the kiln (foreground) and drying sheds. The incline house is centre left; here, clay from the quarry, loaded in a wagon, was hauled up for treatment. The Dudley Canal is on the right of the picture, its route towards Selly Oak marked by telegraph poles. The principal traffic in later years along this part of the Dudley Canal was coal to Smart's Brickworks. (*Birmingham Reference Library*)

5

Grand Union Canal

The Grand Union Canal unites London and the River Thames with Birmingham and the East Midlands. The company came into existence in 1928, and through mergers and purchases between 1929 and 1932 established the lines of canal which are collectively known as the Grand Union Canal today.

Two Birmingham canals form part of the Grand Union System: the Warwick & Birmingham Canal and the Birmingham & Warwick Junction Canal, completed in 1800 and 1844 respectively.

The Warwick & Birmingham Canal was authorised by Act of Parliament in March 1793 and, as the name implies, connected the town of Warwick with Birmingham. The Warwick & Birmingham Canal joins the Digbeth Branch of the BCN and travels via Olton, Knowle and Hatton to Saltisford Basin on the outskirts of Warwick. It was a distance of 22 miles and 5 furlongs, the same length as the original main line of the Birmingham Canal opened in 1772. Construction began at the Digbeth end and by May 1796 had reached Henwood. Work continued through to Warwick, and the Warwick & Birmingham Canal was finally opened to traders in March 1800.

Trade on the Warwick & Birmingham Canal was closely connected to that on the Warwick & Napton Canal, which it met at Budbrooke outside Warwick. The Warwick & Napton was also opened for trade during March 1800. Both canal companies worked closely together. Items which appear in the Warwick & Birmingham committee minute books often appear the next month in the Warwick & Napton's. The Birmingham & Warwick Junction Canal has been described by Charles Hadfield as 'a creature of the two Warwick Canals'. It was promoted jointly by the Warwick & Birmingham and Warwick & Napton Canal Companies, received parliamentary approval in 1840 and was opened in February 1844.

The Birmingham & Warwick Junction Canal joined the Warwick & Birmingham Canal at the bottom of Camp Hill Locks and passed through Saltley and Nechells to Salford Bridge, where a junction was made with the Birmingham & Fazeley Canal. The opening of this canal coincided with the completion of the Tame Valley Canal. Boats destined for the Wednesbury and Bilston iron districts would avoid the heavily used Farmer's Bridge Flight if they passed along the Birmingham & Warwick Junction and Tame Valley Canals.

The first 8 miles of the Warwick & Birmingham and the whole of the Birmingham & Warwick Junction Canals became heavily industrialised. Most notable were three gasworks and a power station, which produced coal and chemical trade for the waterway. There were a number of coal and timber wharves, brick works, corporation depots, and cycle and motor manufacturers. There was also the large BSA works at Small Heath, which manufactured cycles and arms.

Long-distance trade suffered through competition with the railways and all three canal concerns were rarely in profit. Eventually, a joint board of management was appointed to control the total operation. The main commercial carriers were Fellows, Morton & Clayton, whose boats regularly traded between the West and East Midlands and London. The Warwick canals became part of the Grand Union Canal in 1929. The new company set about modernising the route from Napton to Birmingham: towpaths were improved and all the locks widened to take barge traffic, although few, if any, barges came this way. New warehouses were erected at Sampson Road and Warwick Wharf. The Second World War prevented any further improvements, and by the time it had finished in 1945 canal carrying had gone into a serious decline. Motorboat and butty pairs continued to use the Grand Union Canal from London into Birmingham. The Sampson Road, Tyseley and Warwick Wharves were busy with traffic until the end of the 1950s. Many boats on this run belonged to the British Transport Waterways South Eastern Division which controlled these wharves. Commercial carrying went on well into the 1960s, but as elsewhere had become a shadow of its former self. Today, all wharves are closed and the principal traffic is the hire and pleasure boat.

....

Opposite:

1. Lock house
2. Warehouse (*c.* 1810)
3. Warehouse (*c.* 1812)
4. Warehouse (BCN)
5. Warehouse (Grand Junction Carrying Co.)
6. Stables
7. Warwick & Birmingham offices
8. Coal and timber wharves

Old Warwick Wharf and Bar Lock, 1887. There was a toll house and office beside the bar lock. Opposite the lock were carriers' warehouses with covered wharves. The central pair of warehouses was located directly opposite the bar lock with access to a basin that joined the Warwick & Birmingham Canal. The warehouse to the left had a covered basin which communicated directly

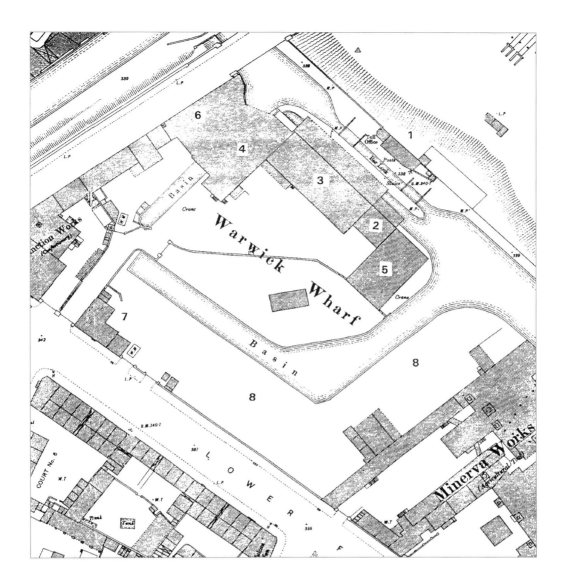

with the Birmingham Canal; the third warehouse, on the right, faced Warwick Wharf Basin. Warwick Wharf was established shortly after the Warwick & Birmingham Canal opened their first piece of waterway to Hay Mills. The first warehouse was constructed on the canal side in about 1810. Pickford & Co. took over these premises in 1812 and completed another warehouse as part of the agreement. Pickford's traded from Fazeley Street until 1847 when they disposed of their London trade to the Grand Junction Carrying Company, who added the warehouse on the right. The Grand Junction Carrying Company gave up carrying in 1876, but their trade was taken over by the London & Staffordshire Carrying Company (L&SCC). The L&SCC was eventually absorbed by Fellows, Morton & Clayton, who were lessors of the warehouses and associated wharves in 1887. The Junction Works occupy the former Grand Junction Carrying Company offices. They share a common entrance with the carriers' wharf. To the right of this entrance are the Warwick & Birmingham Company offices and the entrance to the company part of the wharf. The map does not show the coal and timber merchants' plots, but there was a road around the basin and both had plots, or stations, let to merchants. Every piece of ground was utilised. (*Ordnance Survey: surveyed 1887, published 1889*)

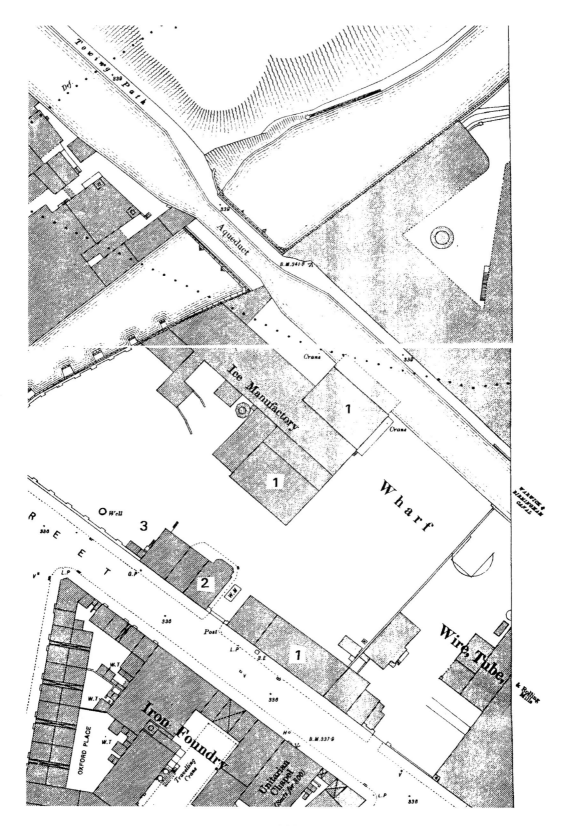

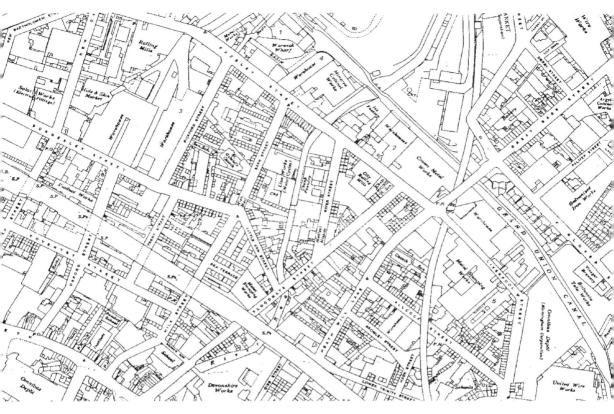

Warwick & Birmingham Canal, Fellows, Morton & Clayton depots, 1936.

1. Original Fellows Morton depot (formerly of the Grand Junction Canal Carrying Company)
2. Fellows Morton 1883 depot
3. Fellows, Morton & Clayton 1912 depot
4. Stables, Liverpool Street
5. Fellows, Morton & Clayton 1936 depot

....

Opposite:

1. Warehouse
2. Offices
3. Later site of cottage

The New Warwick Wharf (1887) was leased from Thomas Gooch in 1836 by the Birmingham Gas Light & Coke Company to build a gasworks. This works was closed in about 1878 and the land reused. The gas holders were demolished but the retort house appears to have been retained as an ice manufactory. The wharf and canal frontage were leased by Fellows, Morton & Clayton in about 1883, the owners then being the Borough of Birmingham. Fellows, Morton & Clayton made several improvements and additions to the wharf. Most notable was a covered basin in the centre of the main wharf. They also added a cottage (1893) and enlarged the offices which faced Fazeley Street (1896). (*Ordnance Survey, 1887*)

Warwick Bar and Old Fazeley Wharf, 1996. This view looks along the canal from the Rea Aqueduct to Warwick Bar. The toll office, where the toll keeper gauged and checked the boats passing through the lock, has gone, but opposite the stop there is still an old canal-side warehouse and canopy. This building formed part of the original warehouse complex used by Pickford & Co. The tall brick building on the left was a warehouse built for Fellows, Morton & Clayton in 1935. This warehouse stands on one side of the filled Warwick Wharf basin and was formerly coal merchants' wharves. There were three entrances into the warehouse which faced the basin; each had roller shutter doors and overhead hoists. In British Waterways days the basin and warehouse were busy with boats unloading metal goods. (*Author's collection*)

New Warwick Wharf, Fazeley Street. Fellows, Morton & Clayton had warehouses at both Old and New Warwick Wharves. Wooden canopies covered most of the canal side at the New Warwick Wharf. In this view the motor *Hawk* and butties *Quebec* and *Usk* (foreground) can be identified. (*National Waterways Museum, Ellesmere Port*)

Above: The former Fellows, Morton & Clayton Offices, Fazeley Street. This 1990s scene has changed little. (*Author's collection*)

Opposite top: Bomb damage, New Warwick Wharf. It is difficult to imagine today the extent of the damage inflicted by wartime bombing. Buildings were destroyed and in some cases the business was lost forever. During the 1950s the bombsite legacy was common throughout the city. Here in Fazeley Street, the Fellows, Morton & Clayton warehouse was damaged and four boats sunk. The *Kildare* (butty, 1913) and *Robin* (motorboat, 1919) were carrying a consignment of tubes, while the *Rover* (motorboat, 1919) and *Grace* (butty) had a cargo of cocoa. Sometimes this image is credited as being at the Typhoo tea factory, but had this been the case the cargoes would have included tea for blending. (*National Waterways Museum, Ellesmere Port*)

Opposite bottom: New Warwick Wharf, Fazeley Street, 1996. The former Fellows, Morton & Clayton Wharf and main warehouse remain, although now converted for other uses: there are a number of small business units and a restaurant on the site. (*Author's collection*)

Above: Adderley Street Gasworks, *c.* 1920. Another view of the gasworks looking along the Warwick & Birmingham Canal towards Engine Lock. The production of coal gas utilises special grades of coal which give the best yield of gas and a gas which burns the brightest. Locally mined coals (sent by boat) gave way to coals from North Wales, the East Midlands and Yorkshire which came by rail. At Adderley Street there were no rail sidings and coal was sent by road from the nearest railhead. Gas making produced a number of by-products which frequently went out by boat. Coke was produced after the coal was burnt to generate the coal gas, and at this time Adderley Street had a coke telpher which carried coke from the retort house over the canal to a coke store. Coke could also be loaded directly into boats from the overhead telpher, and here a boat is positioned under the telpher having just received a load of coke. The canal coke trade supplied blast furnaces, chemical works, foundries and ironworks throughout the region. (*Birmingham Reference Library*)

Opposite top: Camp Hill, Bottom Lock. The Warwick & Birmingham Canal, at Camp Hill, was surrounded by industry that lined the canal on both sides. Below the lock is the junction with the Birmingham & Warwick Junction Canal where boats could turn on towards Salford Bridge. (*RCHS Weaver Collection, ref. 45636*)

Opposite bottom: Adderley Street Gasworks, *c.* 1920. Adderley Street was commissioned by the Birmingham & Staffordshire Gas Light Company in 1842, but was taken over by Birmingham Corporation in 1875. It was the oldest working Birmingham gasworks at the time of this picture. During its existence several alterations were made, including the construction of the No. 2 retort house. This photograph was taken from gasworks property looking across the Warwick & Birmingham Canal at Engine Lock. It shows No. 2 retort house and a water gas plant, the white concrete building in front of it. (*Birmingham Reference Library*)

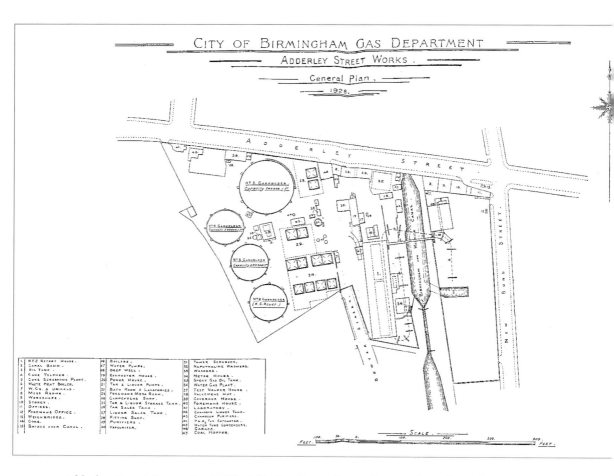

Adderley Street Gasworks, 1928. Adderley Street Gasworks was the only modern gasworks in Birmingham that was not rail served. All raw material and by-products were either carried by canal or road. (*Author's collection*)

Chunk Foundry, Coventry Road. The Chunk Foundry was placed beside the Warwick & Birmingham Canal and had a frontage to the Coventry Road. In this engraving the artist has carefully avoided showing the bridge or lock, which would have been in the foreground from this perspective. Birmingham had several canal-side foundries that cast a range of articles, including those for domestic and industrial purposes. (*Author's collection*)

Above: Warwick & Birmingham Canal, Camp Hill Locks, May 1978. This view from Sandy Lane Lock (No. 54) looks towards Hens Row Lock (No. 53) and the Camp Hill railway bridge. The bridge above the lock carried the railway from Birmingham to Leamington, once a main line busy with express trains to London, Oxford and the west, but now relegated to local train services which run from Moor Street Station to Leamington and Stratford. Many of the waterside buildings seen here have been demolished. This lock was removed in 1990 when the canal was diverted to make way for road development. (*Author's collection*)

Below: A salvage boat heads towards Sandy Lane from Hens Row Lock. During the 1950s salvage boat traffic accounted for much of the remaining horse boat traffic on the local waterways. (*Philip Weaver*)

Sandy Lane New Lock, 1990. The railway, canal and road all crossed at Sandy Lane. During 1990 Sandy Lane became a dual carriageway; as part of this development a new railway bridge was constructed and the canal was diverted. The original canal ran straight from Coventry Road to Sandy Lane, but this was closed off and the old Sandy Lock removed to make way for the new road. A new line of canal was cut that curved away from the Coventry Road, passed under the new road and then swung around beside it. The new lock was made beside the new road. This photograph shows the lock shortly after completion. All Saints' church is in the background. (*Author's collection*)

Iron foundry buildings, Camp Hill Flight, April 1998. A privately owned narrowboat leaves Engine Lock (No. 56) and heads towards the Coventry Road Bridge. The building on the left was the iron foundry. On the right there was a wharf where coal was unloaded for the canal pumping engine. There is still a track or way that leads up to Bowyer Street where the steam engine was located. Pumping is still done at Bowyer Street pumping station, but now the water is recirculated by electric pumps. (*Author's collection*)

Sampson Road Wharves, 1938. The canal wharves at Sampson Road occupied an extensive waterway frontage. Here, a number of narrowboats are moored two abreast. Cranes are transferring cargo to and from the wharf side where metal goods and timber are stacked. Among the narrowboats are motors and butties belonging to the Grand Union Canal Carrying Company. Formed in 1934 from the smaller Associated Canal Carriers, the Grand Union Canal Carriers rapidly increased their fleet of narrowboats. They provided a regular trade between London and Birmingham Sampson Road and Tyseley Wharves before and during the Second World War. (*National Waterways Museum, Ellesmere Port*)

Sampson Road North Warehouse, 1950s. This winter view shows British Waterways narrowboats moored alongside the warehouse and under the canopy. Sampson Road Depot began as a collection of coal merchants' wharves and a cement depot. The first local trade directory reference to the Warwick & Birmingham Canal Company owning the wharf here was in 1888. It became a Grand Union Canal Company wharf in 1929, and from 1948 belonged to the British Transport Commission, South Eastern Division. (*National Waterways Museum, Ellesmere Port*)

Warwick & Birmingham Canal, Sampson Road Depot, April 1998. The former British Waterways Sampson Road Depot (left) remains a canal-side feature on the Warwick & Birmingham Canal. The Camp Hill railway bridge and Camp Hill top lock (No. 52) can be seen in the centre of the picture, while on the right is the self-access storage building which was built as the Bordesley Goods Depot for the Great Western Railway. (*Author's collection*)

Tyseley Wharf, April 1998. There has been a wharf on the site since at least 1834, probably earlier. For many years it was called Yardley Wharf and part of it was used as a coal wharf up until the 1930s. Yardley Wharf was redeveloped by the Grand Union Canal Company to handle steel traffic. After reconstruction it became known as Tyseley Wharf. Recently, the wharf has been fenced off and part of the premises is now occupied by Direct Roofing Supplies. (*Author's collection*)

Stockfield Road Old Bridge, *c.* 1913. The Fellows, Morton & Clayton butty *Beatrice* is passing under the old Stockfield Road Bridge at Yardley. The canal passes through a deep cutting between Stockfield Road and Yardley Road. The canal company had first intended to make a tunnel under the Yardley Road, but decided to open most of the tunnel as a cutting; despite the changes, this waterway under Yardley Road still passes through a short tunnel there. Stockfield Road has been widened since this photograph was taken, and the bridge replaced. (*Birmingham Reference Library*)

Lincoln Road North Bridge, June 1934. The canal wharf at Lincoln Road North, Acocks Green, was used by Wilkins, Son & Summer (coal merchants). Two of their boats can be seen moored beside the wharf beyond the bridge. Coal wharves such as these were once common. Here, coal from collieries on Cannock Chase and Warwickshire would be brought chiefly for domestic sale. (*Birmingham Reference Library*)

Above and opposite: Dredging work is an essential part of canal maintenance. These two views show a steam dredger engaged in filling boats with spoil near Olton. The work shown here was probably part of the widening carried out by the Grand Union Canal Company during the early 1930s. Barges similar to those in the photograph are still used for moving dredging and rubbish. (*Birmingham Reference Library*)

Bolton Street Bridge, 1990. The Birmingham & Warwick Canal is drained while the culvert from Bowyer Street Pump House to the top of Garrison Locks is repaired. (*Author's collection*)

Bolton Street, 1998. Since 1990 there have been a number of changes and improvements to the towpath, partly because of the development of Bordesley Village. New housing has replaced the old factories on the right, and Bolton Street Bridge has been removed. The large factory on the left had been built to make metallic bedsteads for J. Troman. Metallic bedstead making was once an important industry in Birmingham, which is where the bulk of this British trade was based. (*Author's collection*)

Boatbuilding at Saltley Dock, *c.* 1897. Park Wharf, Saltley, became the headquarters for the carrier William Clayton when he moved here from Uxbridge during the mid-1850s. Clayton established a fleet of boats that handled either general merchandise or the by-products of the local gas industry. He used part of Park Wharf to maintain his boat fleet. After William's death in 1882, management of the business passed to Thomas Clayton. Thomas joined in partnership with Frederick Morton and James and Joshua Fellows in 1889, setting up the firm of Fellows, Morton & Clayton. Previously, as Fellows, Morton & Co., their main boatbuilding yard had been at Toll End, Tipton. They now transferred to Park Wharf to build and maintain their West Midland fleet. Boatbuilding was an important local industry, supplying wooden or iron boats to the many carriers who used the local canal network. Often yards were open and exposed to the elements; at Park Wharf workers at least had a roof over their heads. In this view a collection of horse boats, often referred to as butties, are under repair. In the foreground a new steam boat is under construction. In addition to Saltley, Fellows, Morton & Clayton had another boatyard at Uxbridge. They also used other boatbuilders such as Yarwoods from time to time. (*Birmingham Archives, Fellows, Morton & Clayton MS*)

Cactus FMC 329, Park Wharf, Saltley. Fellows, Morton & Clayton had an extensive fleet of motorboats which began with the commissioning of *Linda* in April 1912. *Cactus* was commissioned in May 1935; she had been built by Yarwoods at Northwich but fitted out at Saltley where this picture was taken. *Cactus* was a composite boat – that is, an iron boat with a wooden (elm) bottom. (*Birmingham Archives, Fellows, Morton & Clayton MS*)

Nechells A Power Station, *c.* 1930. Nechells Power Station was also known as Prince's, after Edward, Prince of Wales, who officiated at the opening ceremony in 1923. The new power station was constructed next to the temporary station (1915–16) and a small generating station that supplied the needs of the Tame & Rea District Drainage Board. The generating buildings were situated beside a long basin that joined the Birmingham & Warwick Junction Canal. Here, coal boats were unloaded by overhead telphers. Coal was delivered by boat and railway wagon. (*National Waterways Museum, Ellesmere Port*)

The Canal Basin, Nechells Power Station, *c.* 1923. The new basin was concrete lined and extended under the telphers, which brought the coal slack either into hoppers to feed the boilers or across to a stacking yard on the right-hand side. A side basin also extended beside the generating house where ashes from the boilers were loaded. There was a railway lift bridge which carried a siding across the entrance to the ash basin. There was a similar lift bridge across the main basin entrance for the railway line to the temporary station. (*Birmingham Reference Library*)

6

Canal & River Trust

July 2012 proved to be an important time for waterways in England and Wales, when navigations owned or managed by British Waterways transferred to the Canal & River Trust, taking them out of the public sector and into the hands of a charitable trust. Since 1 January 1947 a large part of the British navigation network has been nationalised, being under the control and financial responsibility of the government. For those waterways in the Birmingham area, the Birmingham Canal Navigations and the Worcester & Birmingham Canal were transferred to the Docks & Inland Waterways Executive (D&IWE) from 1 January that year. The Stratford upon Avon Canal, being railway-owned, passed first to British Railways Western Region and then the D&IWE. With the abolition of the D&IWE and the split in the organisation between docks and waterways, the navigations became first the responsibility of British Transport Waterways, and then (from 1963) British Waterways.

Thus, for nearly fifty years British Waterways has presided over the Birmingham Canal network. As trade declined the importance of the canals did also. An early British Waterways policy was to substitute tolls with licences, resulting in the closure of toll offices. Staff reductions also led to the removal or sale of canal-side cottages. Increasing boating traffic did much to keep the waterways open and has encouraged many improvements to suit boaters' needs. Commercial redevelopment has transformed the water's edge throughout the city centre.

It is now a very different canal-side scene to when British Waterways first took control of these waterways. The first major change was the construction of the International Convention Centre on the site of the old Bingley Hall; then the National Indoor Arena was constructed and this work was followed by Brindley Place. When work started there in 1992, it was estimated to take seven years. Since then other developments have spread out towards Vincent Street, down Farmer's Bridge Locks towards Newhall Street, and along the Worcester & Birmingham Canal towards Bath Row.

The Canal & River Trust came into existence for administrative purposes from 2 July 2012, and an official launch date was made for 12 July. Their Birmingham office is the former Toll Keepers Office at Cambrian Wharf, which is presently manned three days a week, Monday, Wednesday and Friday. In the centre of Birmingham they have inherited a modern waterfront and a popular visitor attraction, as will be seen in the following selection of images.

Above: Gas Street Basin, 2012. Another popular destination for boaters is Gas Street Basin, which has been transformed for the leisure trades. There are bars, restaurants and a constantly changing scene as boats pass through or moor up. (*Author's collection*)

Opposite top: Brindley Place. The scheme that became Brindley Place was first conceived as sketches that bear a remarkable resemblance to what actually was produced. (*Author's collection*)

Opposite bottom: New Main Line, NIA & St Vincent Street Bridge, 2012. The towpaths near the National Indoor Arena (far right) have been bricked and improved since 2000 with the completion of the Symphony Court housing development (left). Further developments created new properties beyond St Vincent Street Bridge and together such structures have transformed the canal side here from an industrial one (of the 1960s) to one of leisure and residential properties. This stretch of waterway is now a popular place for boaters to moor overnight. (*Author's collection*)

Sealife Centre and the ICC. The Sealife Centre has become a popular destination for tourists visiting Birmingham. The power house for the ICC has been a canal-side feature since the ICC was built some twenty years ago. The Birmingham city skyline continues to change and a recent addition (top left) is the new library, which is due to open in September 2013. (*Author's collection*)

Cambrian Wharf Offices, Newhall Branch, July 2012. The former toll office at the top of Farmer's Bridge Locks was converted into offices for British Waterways and is now an office for their successors, the Canal & River Trust. The sign by the lock has been changed to reflect the changing order on English and Welsh waterways. (*Author's collection*)

OTHER TITLES PUBLISHED BY THE HISTORY PRESS

Silent Highways: The Forgotten Heritage of
the Midlands Canals

Ray Shill
978-0-7524-5842-7

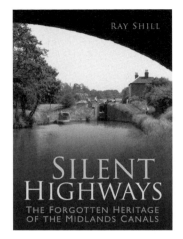

The Canal Pioneers: Brindley's School of
Engineers

Christopher Lewis
978-0-7524-6166-3

Tales from the West Midlands Canals

R.H. Davies
978-0-7524-5500-6

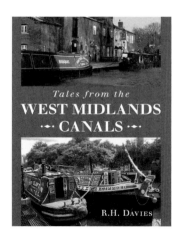

Visit our website and discover thousands of other History Press books.

www.thehistorypress.co.uk